LORD CARLTON
Aristocrat of the Mat

By K.K. Herzbrun
and John Cosper

"Lord Carlton: Aristocrat of the Mat"
Copyright 2018 Eat Sleep Wrestle, LLC
and K.K. Herzbrun

All rights reserved

To my father, the great Lord Leslie Carlton,
from "the Baby"

INTRODUCTION

For much of his adult life, people hated Leo Whippern, and with good reason. Whippern did everything he could to incite the ire and disdain of the masses, carrying himself with all the grace and style of nobility. He cared not whether the people loved him; truth be told, he relished their hate. The fans responded to his pomposity with all the bile and hate afforded to professional wrestlers in a day and age when everyone beyond the locker room, right down to the newspaper reporters who covered the "sport," believed what they saw was real.

Fans and reporters knew him not as the descendant of Hungarian immigrants or even the sailor who served his country from 1944 to 1946, but as Lord Leslie Carlton, a distant relative of the royal family of England. Carlton's legend included service in Her Majesty's armed forces as an officer with the Black Watch Highlanders during World War II. He was a cricket player and tumbler who turned to the mat while stationed in Calcutta, India. After becoming the British Service champion, he turned his attention to those pesky, rebellious former colonies, invading the North American continent to display his dominance over the Queen's former territory.

Carlton strolled to the ring every night with all the pageantry of contemporaries like Gorgeous George, dressed in flowing robes, sporting a monocle, tailed by a faithful servant attending to his master's needs. Carlton looked down on the unwashed masses, on those who should have been grateful that such a regal and lofty fellow would debase himself to be in their presence, and he cared not for the boos and jeers that rained down upon him every night.

All of this back-story, of course, was kayfabe - a carny term that refers to the secrecy that once cast a veil over professional wrestling. Whippern was not English, not a cricket player, and certainly not royalty. He was as American as the men and women who reigned boos down upon him from San Francisco to New York City. Whippern made a great living for his family by becoming the man everyone hated. The more people hated him, the more tickets he sold. The more they wished evil upon him, the more money he could provide for his family.

It was January of 1970 when evil visited Whippern in a way no one, not even the most passionate of fans, would ever wish on someone. Whippern's first wife, an actress from Texas named Peggy Jean Parker, was found dead in her home. She had been choked and stabbed to death in a manner reminiscent of the Biblical story of Abraham, whom God had asked to sacrifice his only son Isaac. While Isaac was spared by God, Peggy Jean's life came to an end. What made the story even more horrific was the identity of the killer: Whippern's only son with Parker, Ricky.

Ricky had a long history with mental illness, and his family had long sought to find treatment for the troubled young man. He had been in and out of mental hospitals four times in the three years leading up to his murder. Ricky also fell into a religious cult during that span, and that's where the crime found its inspiration. Ricky truly believed that God had told him to murder his mother as an act of faith. Newspapers of the day carried a shocking confession from the troubled son.

"God told me that I was an abomination, a wretch, a Judas, but if I had faith, I could raise her."

No one, not even the mighty Lord Carlton, could endure such tragedy without suffering serious implications. It became a major turning point in his story, and the story of his family. No one knows that story better than me, his lordship's only daughter.

My father became an atheist because of the murder. He blamed God for taking away his son, and he refused to allow anything remotely Christian in our home.

That's not to say my father was a bad person. The real Leo Whippern had very little in common with his haughty ring persona, but as good natured as he could be, he was despised by those closest to him: my mother, Leo's second wife, and my older brother, Kitt. The two of them hated my father and demonized him every chance they got. Kitt, a retired physicist with the military, told me he once urinated on my father's grave.

My father was old enough to be my grandfather by the time I was born. I never knew him as a wrestler and my early perception of him was often clouded by my mother and brother. As I grew older, my aunts, uncles, and cousins helped me to get to know him better.

Truth be told, my father was one of the most generous, kind, and loving people I have ever known. He was always giving to the community, supporting charities, and doing whatever he could for friends.

My father was not only generous, but endlessly creative. The fans who booed him and wanted to see him broken in half would have been stunned to know his artistic side. He had a wing of the house just for his art, and he spent much of his days painting away. He painted everything from Jesus to Hulk Hogan. He painted nautical scenes, sports images, and scenes of Americana. He painted Charlie Chaplin, Peter Falk, Lyle Alzado, and his good friend Mel Blanc.

My father had a creative gene that he passed on to me, one that I have embraced and cherished, but my father had scars and wounds that he passed on as well. His second wife, my own mother, compounded his problems with her own mental illness. It was very hard at times growing up in a home where no one was allowed to believe in God and it was terrifying to watch my mother try to destroy my father thanks to her own faults. Yet in spite of it all, I would not trade the upbringing I had as the heir to Lord Carlton. Through all his strengths and weaknesses, he made me who I am today: a creative, chaotic dynamo, a paradox who is both an *avant garde* artist and a conservative believer in Christ.

This is the story of my family: my father, the grandson of Hungarian immigrants, and myself. It's a story about a wrestler, an artist, a father, and a man who lived an incredible life and left behind a beautiful legacy in both oil and flesh.

YOUNG LEO

The weird and wacky world of professional wrestling is full of imposters. For example, the late WWE Hall of Famer Chief Jay Strongbow was not a Native American but a New York Italian. African-American pioneer Seelie Samara was billed as being African royalty. He was actually from the Carolinas, born and raised in the United States. The Hot Scot, Rowdy Roddy Piper, is not from Scotland. He was born in Saskatoon, Saskatchewan, Canada. And Japan's great sumo champion Yokozuna was not even Japanese. He hailed from the proud Anoa'i Samoan wrestling family that includes Rikishi, the Headshrinkers, the Usos, Roman Reigns and The Rock. And Yokozuna's real first name... was Rodney.

All this to say that it should come as no surprise my father was not in fact British, much less British royalty, but in an interesting twist on the norms of pro wrestling, he was the descendant of Hungarian royalty.

My great-grandfather, Barnhard Herzbrun, was a Baron in Hungary. That's not to say he was wealthy and lived in a castle. In fact, he was an English professor at a university. He met my great-grandmother Rosalee when she became a student in his class. He had the title. She had the money. The two were married, and then they fled to America to escape from the on-set of World War I.

The couple settled in Chicago at first, and Professor Herzbrun was sad to learn his skills as an academic were not in demand. He found work as a tailor while in Chicago, and the couple had five children together. They then moved to San Francisco, where Barnhard found work as a presser. Shortly after arriving on the West Coast, Barnhard and Rosalee separated and were divorced.

Rosalee found more success than her husband when she purchased and opened a boarding house. My Great-Uncle Perry often recalled how their mom would sing opera as she cooked meals for her tenants in the kitchen.

The Herzbruns had three sons and two daughters before their marriage ended in divorce. Perry recalled hearing his mother go on and on about how stupid his father was. She didn't do so without proof. One time she took the children into the bedroom and showed them the tightly locked drawer where Barnhard kept his valuables. She then pulled the drawer above the locked one completely from the chest, revealing all of Barnhard's valuables, ripe for the taking.

Barnhard moved to the Sunset district near the beach, but he also rented a room with Rosalee. Despite whatever ills ended their marriage, Barnhard could not resist my great-grandmother's cooking.

My grandmother Kate inherited her mother's musical gifts and was able to translate them into added income for the family. She became the first of us to enter show business when she got a job with the Carlton Sisters, a vaudeville act not to be confused with the country western duo from the Carolinas. The Carlton Sisters were a very popular act on the Pacific Coast, appearing everywhere from Seattle to Los Angeles. Kate's younger brother Perry even got into the act from time to time, appearing on stage with his real sister and her faux sisters.

Kate was only a teenager when she joined the Calton Sisters, and she was still a teen when she met my grandfather. Charles Timothy Wippern owned an opera house in Los Angeles and was the musical director of the First Street Theater in LA. He was also a composer and wrote music for Barnum and Bailey Circus. Wippern and Kate had three children, including my father Leo. The oldest, Arthur, died at 13 of heat stroke.

It's worth noting here that Charles Timothy spelled his last name "Wippern", while my father Leo spelled his Whippern, adding an "H." My father added the "H" in the 1930s, and a quick look at what was going on in the world will tell you why. Wippern was a Germanic name. My cousin GG tracked its origins to the region of Hanover and the town of Hildesheim. As the true motives of the Nazi party came to light, German names became increasingly unpopular in the United States. Just as Harpo Marx changed his real first name from Adolf to Arthur, Leo added an "H" to "Whippern" to distance himself from any association with Nazi Germany.

My brother Kitt did some research on the family name Wippern and found more than a few Wipperns from Hildesheim who were active members of the Nazi party. One of those Wipperns, a man named Georg Wippern, was a field grade officer in the SS who was actively involved in the plundering of German Jews. On the other hand, my cousin GG uncovered a Jesuit priest named Wippern who ended up in a concentration camp, proving that my distant relatives fell on both sides of the razor wire fence!

My father was more in touch with his Hungarian roots because C.T. was not involved in his life for very long. C.T. had a problem with drinking, and Kate grew weary of his boozing early on in the marriage. When my father was 3, Kate told C.T. that if he came home drunk again, she'd leave him. The last time C.T. came home drunk, Kate was waiting for him. Kate, who was 5 feet tall, stood on a chair by the door holding a bottle of wine. When her 6'4" husband staggered through the door, Kate clobbered him with the wine bottle. She took the kids and left. I was told he moved to Illinois.

Kate supported her family by continuing to work as an entertainer, and her children ended up spending a lot of time with their grandmother Rosalee. One of Rosalee's neighbors owned a pet lion, and my father developed a great affection for the lion. I have a great painting he did of a lion hanging in my dining room.

Uncle Perry was the lone adult male in my father's life, and the task of disciplining young Leo fell to him. When the children got out of line, it was Perry who'd spank them. One time my father was begging for a penny and Perry whipped him with a switch and chased him through the house. When Perry found my father hiding under a bed, he yelled "What do you want NOW??"

My father yelled back, "I want a penny!"

The word tenacious comes to mind.

Perry refused to speak Hungarian or German with his parents because they were in the U.S. He became a pilot. He once took Kate up in his plane and then cut the engine and told her they ran out of gas. He did a tail spin down before gunning it back up, and the family said you could hear her screaming from the plane. I think the words crazy and Hungarian go hand in hand. They were all very eccentric.

As an adult, Perry led an adventurous life of his own as the chauffeur to millionaire James L. Flood. Their story is told in the book *The Silver Chauffeur.*

Growing in a Hungarian family infused my father with the wisdom and humor (or lack thereof) Hungarians are known for. Most Hungarian proverbs are dark and negative, tinting Hungarians with a deep sense of sarcasm in their humor. Jerry Seinfeld is a classic example.

My Dad had a Hungarian proverb for every occasion, but there's one I remember best. Whenever anyone asked why he pushed himself so hard physically, he replied, "Because it feels so good when I stop."

Leo was a health nut his whole life. He didn't smoke, he didn't drink, and he didn't do drugs. That made him a bit of an oddball when he later went into the wild world of pro wrestling, but it probably lengthened his career.

His devotion to good health can be traced back to age twelve, when my father spent seven months in the hospital. A minor injury that occurred when my father was playing ball led to a severe case of blood poisoning. This was an archaic time in medical history, and my father spent a great deal of time strapped to a board at an angle for draining. He became very frail and weak.

Young Leo Whippern was not given much chance of survival, but in the end his life was spared. His Uncle Perry stepped in and volunteered to give the boy an arm to arm blood transfusion, and shortly after, my father went home. Perry often took credit for my father's recovery as well as his strength. He very likely saved Leo's life.

After that incident, my father devoted himself to clean living, healthy eating, and physical activity. He never wanted to be sick or weak or helpless again, and that drove him all his life. He never drank, smoked or did drugs, but became an advocate for clean healthy living.

Leo had a serious mistrust of doctors, especially chiropractors whom he referred to as "chiro-quackers." He never went to the doctor, but as vigilant as he was about healthy living, he rarely needed a doctor.

Leo was very black and white about a lot of things in life. When he was around nine years old an earthquake hit the California coast. It was powerful enough to crack the ground and open up a few of the graves in a cemetery where Dad used to run and play. While running through the graveyard, he paused to look down into a crack in the Earth, where he saw the remains of a long dead soul still in the grave. It was then, my father later told me, that he stopped believing in life after death.

I don't know if that's really when my father lost his faith, but that's how he was. Black and white. One moment, one experience, and his mind was made up. Period.

Another major milestone happened when my father was nine. A lady came to the door looking for donations for the San Francisco School for the Arts, now the San Francisco Art Institute. My grandmother wasn't home, so Leo answered the door. Leo was already an avid artist, and after asking a number of questions of the lady, he asked if she wanted to see some of his work.

The lady from the art school agreed, expecting to see the usual doodles of a small child. The woman was very astonished by what she saw. She thought so much of my father's work she made plans to return when his mother was home.

My grandmother was shocked by the woman's reaction to Leo's talent. Even though he was only nine, the woman offered Leo a full scholarship to the art school. He became the youngest student in the history of the school.

Leo dove into his art education with a great deal of passion. Three years later, when he committed himself to being healthy and strong, he brought the same level of commitment to his fitness drive.

Young Leo became a dedicated athlete, and he excelled at swimming. He earned a mention in the *Oakland Tribune* in 1936 as a top competitor for the Fleishhacker Swimming Club, competing in the two-mile Golden Gate Swim along Neptune Beach.

Leo took up wrestling and boxing at the YMCA and the Olympic Club in San Francisco. At age seventeen he won a Golden Glove championship. But Leo, always conscientious about his health, realized that boxing was not for him in the long term. Sports medicine wasn't what it is now back then, but Leo was shrewd enough to know if he wanted to keep his brain intact, he should find a new line of work.

That's when Leo Whippern decided to become a professional wrestler.

Above: My great-grandfather, Baron Herzbrun.
Below: My great-grandmother Rosalee, the Baroness.

Above: My grandmother Kate and her brother Perry.
Below: The Carlton Sisters.

Kate Whippern, Leo's mother and my grandmother.

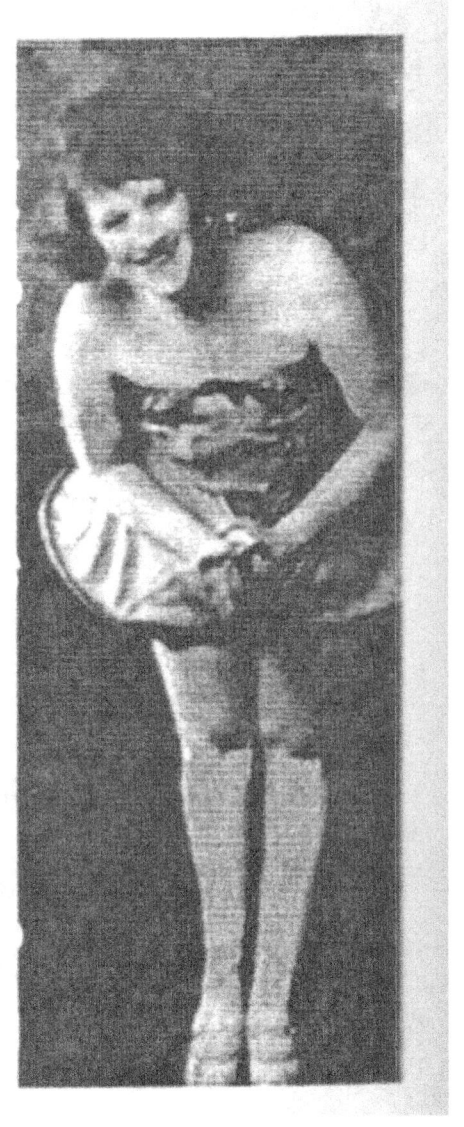

Kate in one of her dance outfits.

Kate's children: Arthur in the back, Paula, and young Leo, my dad.

Dad with his sister Paula.

Dad as a young athlete.

TUG CARLSON IS BORN

I don't know whether my father knew that wrestling was staged when he chose wrestling over boxing. At that time most Americans believed wrestling to be completely on the level, but just like today, it was a staged form of entertainment rather than a pure athletic competition as it had been nearly from the beginning.

In its earliest days, pro wrestling became fixed because promoters saw money in rigging the matches. Wrestlers would travel from town to town, fabricating rivalries with other wrestlers who were actually their partners in crime. One guy would move into town and establish himself make as the fan favorite, later known as a babyface. His partner would roll into town and answer an open challenge, taking on the role of the "heel." If they played it right, they could make a ton of money off one match, and if that match ended in a controversial manner, they could make even more money from the marks (fans) who wanted to see the inevitable rematch.

"I didn't want to have a career of being hit in the head so much," he once told me. "I wanted to wrestle." He knew that wrestling offered him more of a chance for longevity, but he confessed that he was also drawn in by the flamboyant, artistic side of the sport. His family was full of entertainers, and Leo was born to entertain.

When my father first broke into the business, he was on the side of goodness and right. In his earliest shows he was billed as Leo Carlson, which was later changed to Tug Carlson and later Swede Carlson. Swede Carlson was pitched, not surprisingly, as a Swedish wrestler, but other promoters pitched Carlson as being Irish. It all depended on where he was in the country and what the makeup of the promoter's core audience was. Promoters still do this sort of shenanigans today. Terry Bollea became Terry "Hulk" Hogan because Vince McMahon, Sr., was in need of an Irishman.

Military men were very fashionable in wrestling at the time, so Tug Carlson became a sailor. Depending on where he was in the country he was billed as hailing from anywhere between his real hometown of San Francisco, California; to the land-locked city of Des Moines, Iowa; to the land of a thousand lakes in Minneapolis, Minnesota. Again, it all depended on where Dad was working, who he was working for, and what would sell tickets.

He was a well-built man at 6'2" weighing 225 pounds with curly blonde hair and handsome features, a natural babyface. My cousin GG, who was just a boy when "Uncle Tug" got into the wrestling business, called him Uncle Choo Choo because his mother bragged that my father could lift up a train.

Tug Carlson's earliest recorded match, according to wrestlingdata.com, took place on April 8, 1941 at the Coliseum Bowl in San Francisco. Leo Carlson scored a win over Jack Gacek that night and a week later defeated Jack Kojut. In week three he fought Gordon McKenzie to a time limit draw.

Tug wrestled sparsely the rest of the year. Professional wrestling was in the midst of resurgence, having suffered a bit through the Depression, but the high hopes were tempered with the ever looming prospect of entry into World War II. The most notable feud my father had during 1941 took place in September when he twice lost to Wild Bill Longson. Born in Utah in 1906, Longson is often credited as being the man who perfected the modern day role of the heel in wrestling as well as popularizing the pile driver finish. A durable athlete who wrestled for nearly three decades, Longson would be the primary torch bearer for pro wrestling and the heavyweight championship during the war as he was medically unable to enlist.

My father stuck to the West Coast in his early years, fighting in San Francisco, Los Angeles, Pasadena, Fresno, and other California cities before shooting up to the Oregon territory. In July of 1942 he lost to Sandor Szabo, a fellow Hungarian who became a huge draw on the West Coast and won multiple championships in his 34-year career. In October of that same year he faced off against Wee Willie Davis, a beast of a man at more than 400 pounds who also became a movie star.

Carlson developed a reputation early on for his power and strength. He was called a rough-houser and a ruffian. The *Medford Mail Tribune* called him one of the "best-liked pachyderms ever to show in this part of the country." He started out playing the good guy, but Tug Carlson learned early on how to get rough and dirty. During his stay in Oregon, Carlson was sometimes known for cowering and ducking between the ropes to escape a beating and regroup, while at other times he was known for his "less than scientific" tactics in the ring. One reporter described a

Tug Carlson match as looking more like boxing than wrestling with all the fisticuffs that took place. Still, Tug added a few high-impact maneuvers to his arsenal, including the flying tackle, the flying leg scissors, and the airplane spin, in which he would hoist his opponent over his shoulders in a fireman's carry and spin him in circles before dropping him to the mat.

In March of 1943 Tug had a less than scientific bout with Pierre DeGlane in Bakersfield. DeGlane, playing the heel, grabbed a wadded up piece of paper from the floor and tried to shove it down Tug Carlson's throat. This went on for the better part of seventeen minutes, driving the fans mad as DeGlane kept his comical assault hidden from the referee. Tug finally popped his opponent on the right jaw a few times and hit him with a body press for the win.

Carlson had a unique feud in 1943 with Wild Red Berry, one of the most verbose talkers of his day and a man who loved to rile the crowd with his gift for words. Tug was working heel along with Berry, and the two were paired up for a tag match. Berry bailed out during the conflict, leaving Carlson to do all the work. It was a classic heel tactic that created some tension between the two men in the eyes of the fans.

When the two were paired again three weeks later, fans showed up en masse to see if the two would co-exist or implode. Carlson and Berry did not disappoint, and the two men ended up brawling more with each other more than with their opponents. The referee tried to maintain control and even ordered the men into the ring for a fourth fall, which they lost.

A month later Carlson and Berry met in the ring for another tag match. This time Berry was teamed with former rival George Dusette while Carlson teamed with Danny McShain. Carlson kept a piece of tape on his person that he used to remove eyebrows and other body hairs from his opponents. Berry and Dusette went after the tape and then Carlson himself.

Tug survived to take the first fall before turning the match over to his tag partner. McShain took a beating from Dusette and Berry and lost the fall, prompting Carlson to eject him from the ring and tell him he wanted a new partner- specifically, he said, a four-year-old child.

The third fall things really got ugly. Fans became so enraged with Tug they actually stormed the ring. The referee and the PA announcer were both entangled in the fracas as people tried to get their hands on my father. Dusette scored the final pin by slamming Carlson into the ring post and stepping on his chest for the three count.

The two pairs met one more time to settle matters between them once and for all. It was another two out of three falls match and once again, Berry and Dusette took the upper hand. The Bakersfield reporter said that Berry "walloped Carlson until he was as groggy as a pet coon feeding on whiskey mash."

In another late 1943 match, Tug Carlson took a sock to the jaw from a fan near ringside. It was in Bakersfield again, and after the incident hit the papers, Carlson offered $500 as a bet to the unknown man who belted him if he would dare to challenge Carlson in the ring. He offered $50 to one man who might have known the attacker's identity, but the man, "who resides in this community and pays his taxes and tries to get along with his neighbors, no matter how ornery they are," refused to talk.

"Tug" became more than just a catchy name that appeared in the wrestling fliers. My father took to boating and sailing and even had a houseboat that he named "Tugboat."

His connection to the sea became even stronger in the summer of 1944, when the selective service finally called his number. Leo Whippern was drafted into the Navy, but he was very anti-war and did not want to go. He pled conscientious objector, and when that didn't work, he went to a doctor friend, who was of German descent, and asked him to write a letter to try and get him out of the service. While he was unable to avoid serving, he managed to get out of a trip to Europe and was sent to the Pacific theater.

Leo served in the Merchant Marines and was stationed on Guam. Duty to his country may have taken him away from his burgeoning career for the last two years of the war, but Leo found a way to bring the mat game to himself by organizing wrestling shows for the troops in Guam India.

"Tug traveled the whole world in the Merchant Marines," says Johny Andriolo, who became close friends with my father and mother in the mid sixties. "He wrestled the champion of India, Egypt. Anywhere he went, he wanted to wrestle the top guy, and he always won."

Fact or fiction, Tug's experiences in the Merchant Marines would become part of the legend of Lord Carlton. It was in India that Lord Leslie Carlton laid claim to the British wrestling title. There's no newspaper record of the match which reportedly took place in Ceylon, and it's entirely possible the championship was merely a fabrication to further the legend of my father's future alter ego.

Another story lost to time, sadly, is how my father ended up going AWOL by accident. He was on a ship that was lost at sea for a short time, and somehow he was reported AWOL. My cousin Ritchie knew the tale and told it to me. He's gone now, and I wish I could remember more of the details.

The war ended officially on September 2, 1945, when the Japanese formally surrendered. Four months later, Leo Whippern was given an honorable discharge from the service, releasing him to return to life as a self-employed professional wrestler.

NOTICE OF SEPARATION FROM U. S. NAVAL SERVICE
NAVPERS-553 (REV. 8-45)

934-54-37 WHIPPERN, Leo B Specialist (Athletic) 2/c (T) SV-6 USNR	2327 Shoemaker, California
3052 S. Norton St Los Angeles, California Los Angeles County	Honorable Same as #4
Race: W Sex: M Marital: S Citizen: Yes	9-13-14 San Francisco, Calif
Registered: Yes San Francisco, S.F.Co.Calif	Reseda, California
Enlisted Date: 7-25-44 7-25-44	7-25-44 01-05-16 Atlanta, Georgia
Promoted boxing & wrestling shows, supervised building of Gymnasiums.	AS, S2/c, Sp(A)3/c(T), Sp(A)2/c(T)
NTS(P.I.) Bainbridge, M.D. 8	NOB, Naval Barracks-Navy 926
NSI 0 2-46 7.10 Yes	
244.96 146.30 PAID	B. D. Pollock Lt. (jg) 520-001

Remarks:
Point System
Asiatic-Pacific
American
Victory Ribbon

FRED O. GOODELL
LIEUTENANT USNR

Self-Employed	From 1930 To 1944	Wrestler
Same as #38., California.	Yes, Undecided as to type.	
8 4 0 - General	Art School-2 years German-1 yr.	
	Spanish	

1-10-46

Leo Brooks Whippern

TO: BUREAU OF NAVAL PERSONNEL

After a recent move, I discovered my father's discharge papers from the Navy. He enlisted in Atlanta, Georgia on July 25, 1944 and was discharged honorably on January 10, 1946. The document lists my father as "self-employed" from 1930 to 1944 as a promoter of boxing and wrestling shows as well as a builder of gymnasiums. His art school is listed under vocational training.

Newspaper cartoon featuring the great Tug Carlson. I have the metal stamp for this cartoon in my memorabilia collection.

WRESTLING

TOMORROW NIGHT

WEDNESDAY
December 15, 1943

2201 V Street   8:30 o'Clock

RETURN BATTLE
TEAM-TAG MATCH
WINNER TAKE ALL

MAIN EVENT
Two Out of Three Falls to a Finish

Wild Red Berry
George Dusetti

Versus

Tug Carlson
Danny McShain

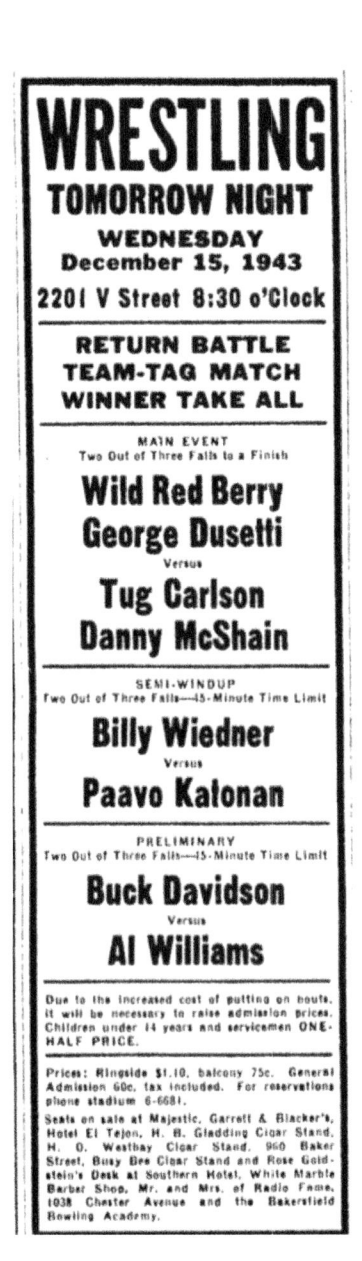

SEMI-WINDUP
Two Out of Three Falls—45-Minute Time Limit

Billy Wiedner

Versus

Paavo Katonan

PRELIMINARY
Two Out of Three Falls—45-Minute Time Limit

Buck Davidson

Versus

Al Williams

Due to the increased cost of putting on bouts, it will be necessary to raise admission prices. Children under 14 years and servicemen ONE-HALF PRICE.

Prices: Ringside $1.10, balcony 75c. General Admission 60c, tax included. For reservations phone stadium 6-6681.

Seats on sale at Majestic, Garrett & Blacker's, Hotel El Tejon, H. B. Gladding Cigar Stand, H. O. Westbay Cigar Stand, 960 Baker Street, Busy Bee Cigar Stand and Rose Goldstein's Desk at Southern Hotel, White Marble Barber Shop, Mr. and Mrs. of Radio Fame, 1038 Chester Avenue and the Bakersfield Bowling Academy.

Ad for the rematch between Berry and Dusette vs. Carlson and McShain.

Autographed photo of Tug Carlson from my personal collection. There aren't many legitimate autographs of my father. He was a heel, after all!

TEXAS BOUND

Tug Carlson returned as a war hero, as all the boys did, and in 1946 he resumed his career. He started back with a match against his old rival Wee Willie Davis on January 20 in San Bernardino. The local paper hyped him as a former world championship contender, but for the most part the World War II veteran found himself in the curtain jerker. (That's wrestler-speak for the opening match of the night, or the first to jerk back the curtain.)

The secret to longevity in the old territory days was to keep moving from town to town. You stayed long enough in one place to get hot but not so long that the people got tired of you. Those who were able to work both sides, as a good guy and bad guy, could double the length of their stay in a city by switching sides when it was normally time to leave. They would still leave town while they were hot, often thanks to a "loser leaves town" stipulation, so that when and if they ever returned, they would be welcomed with open arms or booed like never before. After working California for a few months, Carlson packed his bags and moved on to the great state of Texas.

Promoter Jerry Schultz hyped Carlson as a speedy, scientific wrestler from the West Coast, but less than a week after his arrival, he was billed as a native of Stockholm instead of San Francisco. He made his debut against local favorite Jim Casey in Galveston. The two went the 45 minute time limit, with both men scoring a pin before time ran out.

Tug worked shows in Galveston Waco, and the world famous Sportatorium in Dallas that spring, he was enormously popular with the fans and quickly climbed to the top of the cards. During a match with Frank Taylor, fans streamed to the edge of the ring every time Taylor got Carlson on the ropes, urging on their hero.

His first main event came against a familiar foe from California, Jules Strongbow. Strongbow, outweighed Carlson by 90 pounds, and he used his size to his advantage, tossing Carlson around and eventually out of the ring. His roughhouse tactics cost him the first fall, and Carlson's brilliant skill helped him to finish off Strongbow for a two falls to none victory.

The heroic Carlson turned villain for his next opponent, former navy wrestling champion Bobby Bruns. Fans came expecting a tactical affair but were treated to an out and out brawl as Carlson resorted to head butts and tossing his opponent out of the ring, a move that cost him the final fall.

Carlson also battled Leroy McGuirk and Ernie Dusek in Texas, but his biggest match came on June 17 when he met the original Nature Boy, Buddy Rogers. Rogers was the Texas Heavyweight Champion at the time, and Carlson's former opponent Leroy McGuirk was the number one contender. But on June 13, promoter Jerry Shultz announced that Carlson had persuaded McGuirk to give up his title shot. McGuirk was working in Mexico City at the time, and Carlson offered to give McGuirk his pay for the title match if he stayed in Mexico City and let Carlson take the title shot.

The bout was set for a 90 minute time limit, two out of three falls. Shultz expressed some disappointment at not getting the Rogers-McGuirk match up he originally booked, but the fans and press were eager to see a brawler like Carlson get his hands on the champ.

The match was described as one of the roughest ever seen on the island of Galveston. Tug Carlson fell behind seven seconds into the match. Carlson had his back turned to Rogers when the bell rang and was too busy playing to the crowd to see the champ racing up behind to put him in a cradle for the first pin.

The early pin fall brought out the darker side in Tug Carlson, who "slugged, choked, and butted Rogers' head against the rope turnbuckles until the champion dropped half-dazed to the mat." Carlson's brutality earned him a three count, and the match was tied.

Rogers and Carlson unleashed all their dirty tricks in the third fall. Carlson caught Rogers low on the body and the champion went to the mat, grabbing his crotch and lolling about in pain. The low blow led to a disqualification, giving the victory to the champ, but no sooner did the bell ring Rogers was on his feet, laughing and racing up the aisles. The ref had fallen for the Nature Boy's ruse, and Carlson came up empty handed.

Tug's last great rivalry during his stint in Texas was with another legend in the making, Freddie Blassie. Blassie was not yet the "Classy" blonde heel that he would become. He was a former sailor like my father, and he brought an impressive resume with him to Texas, including a 45 minute draw with former champion Bronko Nagurski.

Blassie won the match in two straight falls, despite some dirty dealings from Carlson. Jerry Shultz had a new hero to sell to the fans, and it was time for my father to move on.

Carlson left a lasting impression on the fans in Texas. Galveston sports columnist A.C. Becker, Jr., posted a column on July 17, 1946, about what it took to become a star in the professional wrestling game. Becker asserted that you either had to be a great scientific wrestler with a great reputation or a great villain. Tug Carlson was singled out as being the latter, the kind of wrestler with enough villain in him to move the turnstiles at the matches.

Becker cited promoter Jerry Shultz as saying that Carlson had a terrific following in Texas. Any time Tug appeared on the card, the fans would pack the house, eager to boo the villain and cheer for his opponent. But Becker was quick to point out that Carlson might not be such a draw if he tried to be the good guy.

"If Carlson was anything but a meanie," said Becker, "His following would be meager."

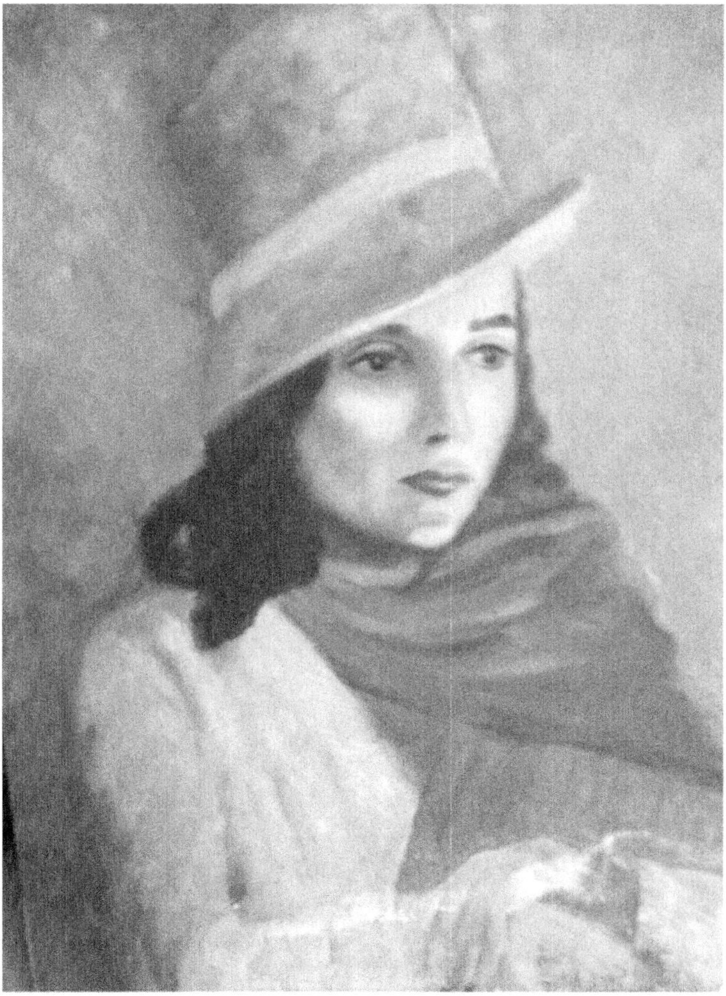

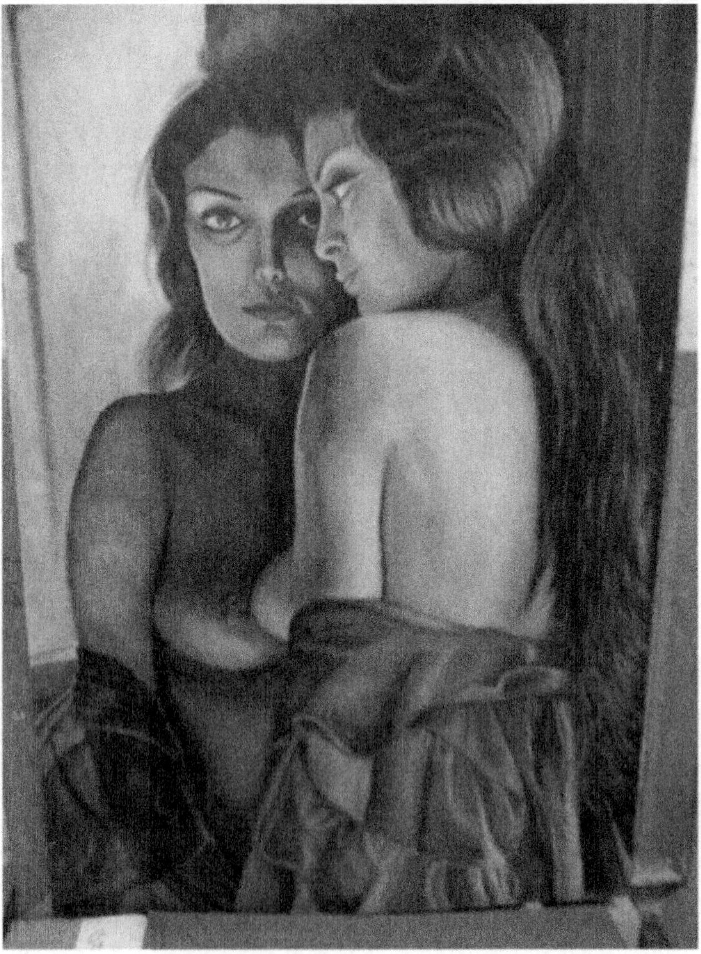

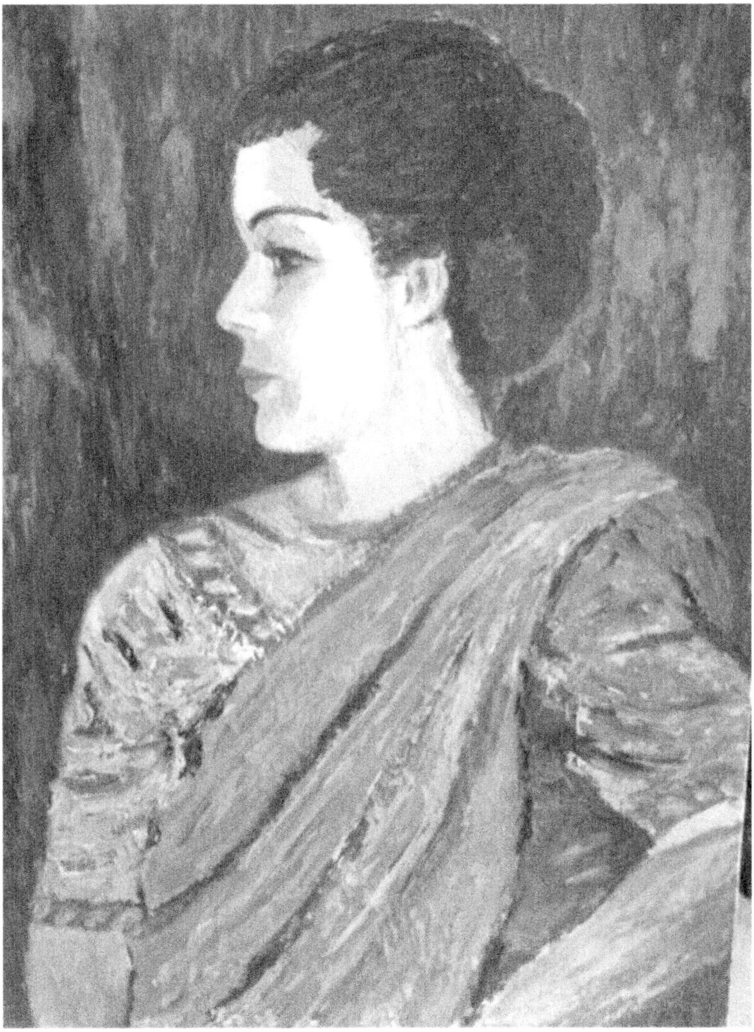

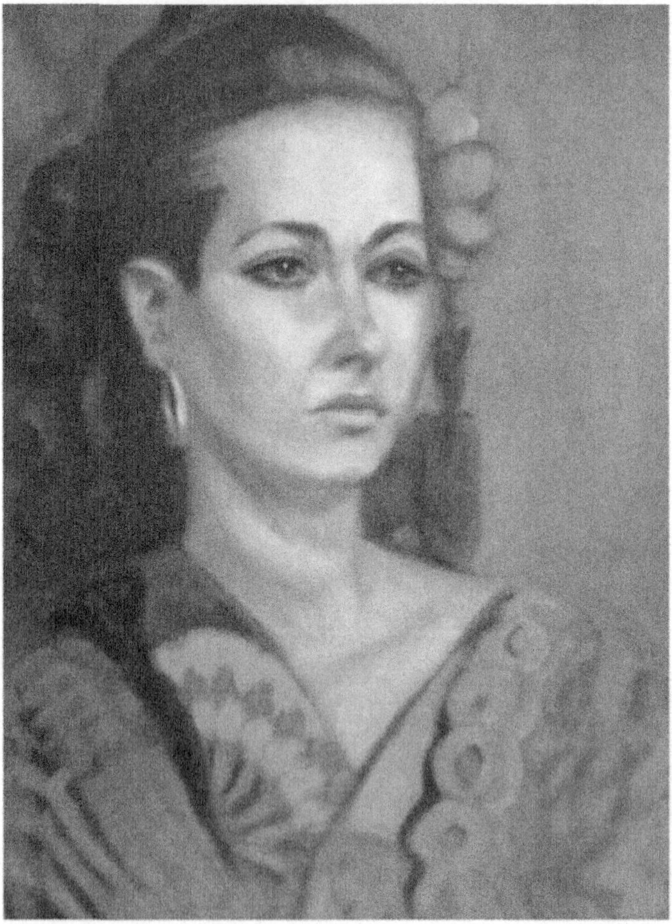

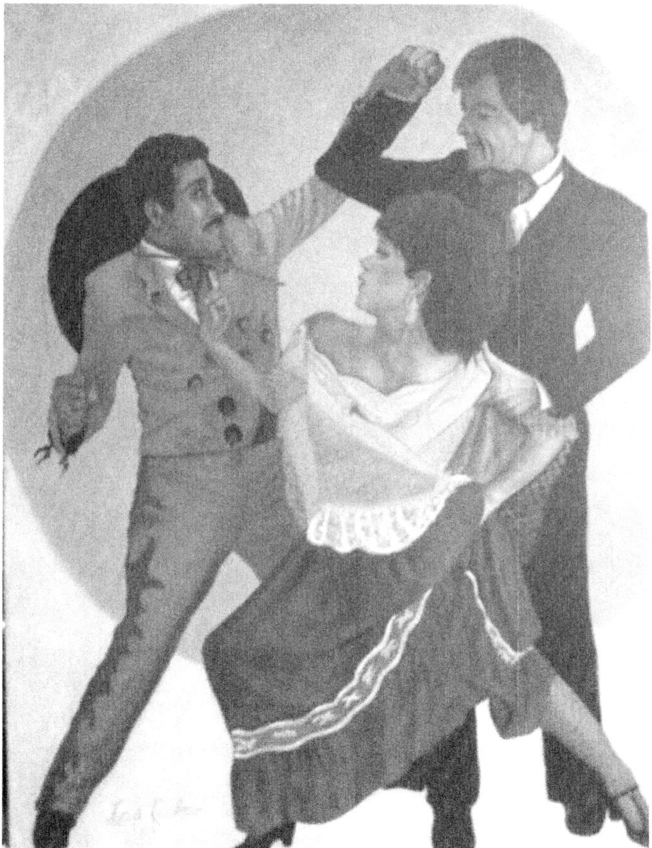

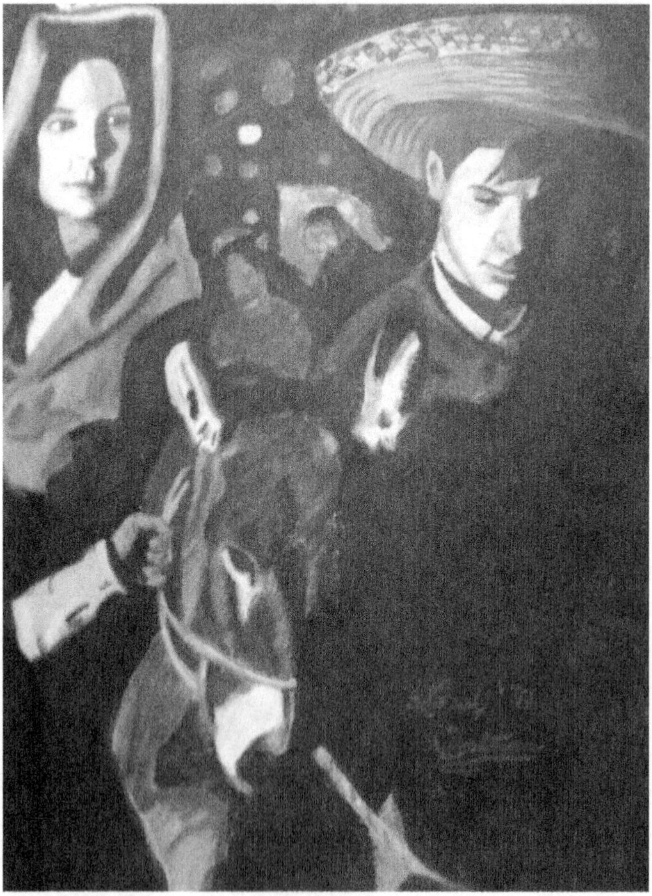

NUMBER ONE CONTENDER

Tug Carlson spent some time in North Carolina before returning to California in September for a two month stint, facing old foes and new. Then, for some inexplicable reason, he decided to head north just as the weather was getting cold, traveling through Canada and the northern United States.

In November of that year, Tug went to Kalispell, Montana. He worked as a referee for the matches at the McIntosh Opera House, and fans appreciated his hands on style when he would get physical with wrestlers who didn't heed his warnings.

Tug wrestled a match in Kalispell that was, at the time, a true rarity. Tug's opponent was King Kong Clayton, a native of Ohio and one of the very few African-Americans working as a full-time wrestler. Most promoters at the time would not allow blacks to wrestle whites. They could battle Asians, Mexicans, and fellow African-Americans, but an in-ring confrontation with white wrestlers was taboo. There's no record of who won the match, but the fact that Tug Carlson took the match puts him at the vanguard of those who helped to break the color barrier in the sport he loved. He would later face other African-American stars including Seelie Samara and The Black Panther Jim Mitchell, whom he also tagged with in California.

Tug worked against Lord Albert Mills in Seattle, Washington in January of 1947. He was part of a group of "new blood" the promoters were bringing into the territory, and Tug reportedly was telling everyone he wanted to settle down in the Pacific Northwest.

Around that same time, Tug began working across the Canadian border in Lethbridge, Alberta. The sailor from San Francisco, as he was now billed, was enormously popular with the female fans in the Great White North, and despite the cold weather, the Alberta promotion was having trouble finding enough seats for the fans in the Roller Barn. Promoter Bus Murdoch erected new bleachers in February to accommodate the demand that Carlson and the other regulars had created.

A February 20 match against Texan Jim "Riot Call" Wright ended in a riot when the referee awarded victory to Wright in a disqualification. The main event was tied at one fall a piece and was already a classic with both men using every dirty trick in the book. Carlson hit Wright with a series of body slams and locked him in a hold. Sensing that Wright had nearly had enough, referee Ralph Robinson forced Carlson to break the hold. Carlson was enraged and grabbed the referee to toss him into the front row. Robinson got himself together, slipped back in the ring, and raised Wright's hand, declaring him the winner.

Carlson decked the referee, and all Hell broke loose. Referees from the back raced to Robinson's aid as fans bombarded the ring with popcorn, paper bags, newspapers, gloves, and ladies shoes. Tug Carlson's fans stormed into the ring and lifted their hero's hand in victory, capping a wild night of wrestling.

As usually happens in these cases, the melee led to a rematch. This time, promoter Murdoch appointed two referees for the bout to "insure that Carlson receives a fair and just decision." The rematch proved to be even more brutal than the first, with Wright playing dirty from the opening bell. When Carlson tried to tie up the lace on one of his boots in mid-bout, Wright laid into him and refused to heed the ref's call to back off. Wright was disqualified, and Carlson was declared the winner.

When the weather warmed up, Tug Carlson headed south to work the central plains states. Tug crossed paths with the Duseks quite often. Known as the Riot Squad, the Duseks were one of the earliest factions in professional wrestling, laying the groundwork for future alliances like the Four Horsemen, the Hart Foundation, Degeneration X, and the NWO. They were heat magnets, hated wherever they went, and the kind of men that made lovable heroes out of whomever stood in the opposite corner.

It was during this period of his life that my father got married for the first time. I have no record of a wedding date or any details on how they met, but I can tell you that Leo Whippern married his first wife Peggy in Montana in 1947. Their only son Ricky was born in San Francisco some time in 1948. They separated when Ricky was little, and my father got custody of Ricky when the boy was only eight.

My cousin GG recalls his parents telling him not to say anything to anyone about his cousin Ricky. It was all very hush hush for some reason, as if my father had taken Ricky and didn't want Ricky's mother to find out.

My father never said much about Peggy, at least nothing much that was positive. He would lament to me that she began her day with caffeine and aspirin and end each day with ice cream for dinner. I heard whispers from other relatives that she was an alcoholic, but never having met her, I can't say if that was true or not. He was so thorough in purging her from his life, I can't even tell you when their marriage ended.

Marriage wasn't the only milestone my father achieved in 1947. Over the summer Tug Carlson finally got a vote of confidence from the powers-that-be when he wrestled a series of matches against Orville Brown. One of the biggest stars of his time, "Roughhouse" Orville Brown, was a native of Kansas and the reigning Midwest Wrestling Association champion. A year after his rivalry began with my father, Brown helped to establish the National Wrestling Alliance.

Tug Carlson and Orville Brown met for the first time in a two out of three falls match in Wichita, Kansas on July 7, and then faced off three more times for the title in Kansas City before the month was out. Tug Carlson came up the loser every time.

Brown and Carlson resumed their battles two months later in St. Joseph, Missouri. They met twice, on September 19 and 26, in St. Joseph, and Brown won both confrontations.

Wrestling titles do not change hands based on merit and skill, of course. They change based on what WWE's Triple H might say is "best for business." Orville Brown was a proven draw, a talented, believable champion who sold out arenas wherever he went. As talented as my father was, he was still just six years into the business. It was an honor just to be in the ring with a champion the caliber of Orville Brown, and it was always a boost for one's career. But getting the title shot didn't always translate to becoming world champion.

That being said, my father did get his moment of glory. On December 19, 1947 in St. Joseph, Missouri, Tug Carlson defeated Orville Brown to become the Midwest Wrestling Association Heavyweight Champion. My father proudly carried that title for a whopping seven days before doing the honors and dropping it back to Brown on December 26.

At least he got to be champion for Christmas, right?

My father had finally reached the top of the business he loved, but there was no where else for him to go. He met Brown twice more for the NWA World Heavyweight Championship in January of 1949, but he came out the loser just as he had before.

Dad continued to travel the country working the middle card and the occasional tag match, but he must have known the writing was on the wall for the Tug Carlson.

Orville Brown's days as world champion came to an end later in 1949. On November 1, Brown suffered career-ending injuries in a car accident. Brown was in talks to do a title-unification match with Lou Thesz, but after the accident, Brown was forced to surrender his title.

With the passing of the torch from Brown to Thesz, my father realized Tug Carlson had gone as far as he could go in the business. My father was frustrated. He loved wrestling and he was not ready to give it up, but the last thing he wanted was to spend the rest of his career working mid-card matches. If he wanted to stay at the top of the card where the real money was, he was going to have to do something to make himself stand out. The wrestling business was already overflowing with sailors and soldiers, and with his black trunks and good looks, there was nothing about Tug Carlson to make him stand out.

Perhaps it was a tag match in the fall of 1948 that provided the inspiration my father needed. It was October 7, at the Long Beach Municipal Auditorium, which Tug and another ground-breaking performer teamed up for a tag match. Their opponents were a pair of masked heels, named the Golden Terror and a villainous foreigner named Hans Schnabel.

Bronko Nagurski had been advertised for the tag match. Carlson was listed as facing Lord Blears, but when the former Chicago Bear was a no-show, Carlson was bumped up to the main event. His tag partner was a man who, like himself, had been the everyman-type babyface struggling to stand out from the crowd. After nearly a decade, the man once known as George Wagner had fully evolved into a persona tailor made for the new television audience: "Gorgeous George".

Tug Carlson's debut in Galveston for Jerry Shultz, 1946.

Sunday ad for the title shot against Buddy Rogers in Galveston, Texas.

Tug Carlson having a rough time against Jim Casey.
Photos courtesy of Myrtle Casey.

Ad for the clash between Tug Carlson and African-American wrestler King Kong Clayton in Kalispell, Montana.

PRO-HEAVYWEIGHT
WRESTLING
2 Main Events—2 Out of 3 Falls

Tug Carlson vs. Jim "Riot Call" Wright

TWO REFEREES HAVE BEEN ORDERED BY THE LETHBRIDGE WRESTLING COMMISSION FOR THIS MATCH TO WATCH THE UNETHICAL TACTICS OF JIM "RIOT CALL" WRIGHT AND TO INSURE THAT CARLSON RECEIVES A FAIR AND JUST DECISION.

Dick Bishop vs. Earl McCready

Bond has been posted to guarantee Bishop's appearance. Snappy preliminaries.

THURSDAY, MARCH 6 AT 8.30 P.M.
IN THE
ROLLER BARN, Lethbridge
Admission: All one price, $1.00

Advance ticket sale now on at Blenner-Hassett and Smith's and the Roller Barn

GET YOUR TICKETS EARLY AND AVOID STANDING IN LINE

The rematch between Tug Carlson and Jim "Riot Call" Wright.

Tug Carlson in 1947

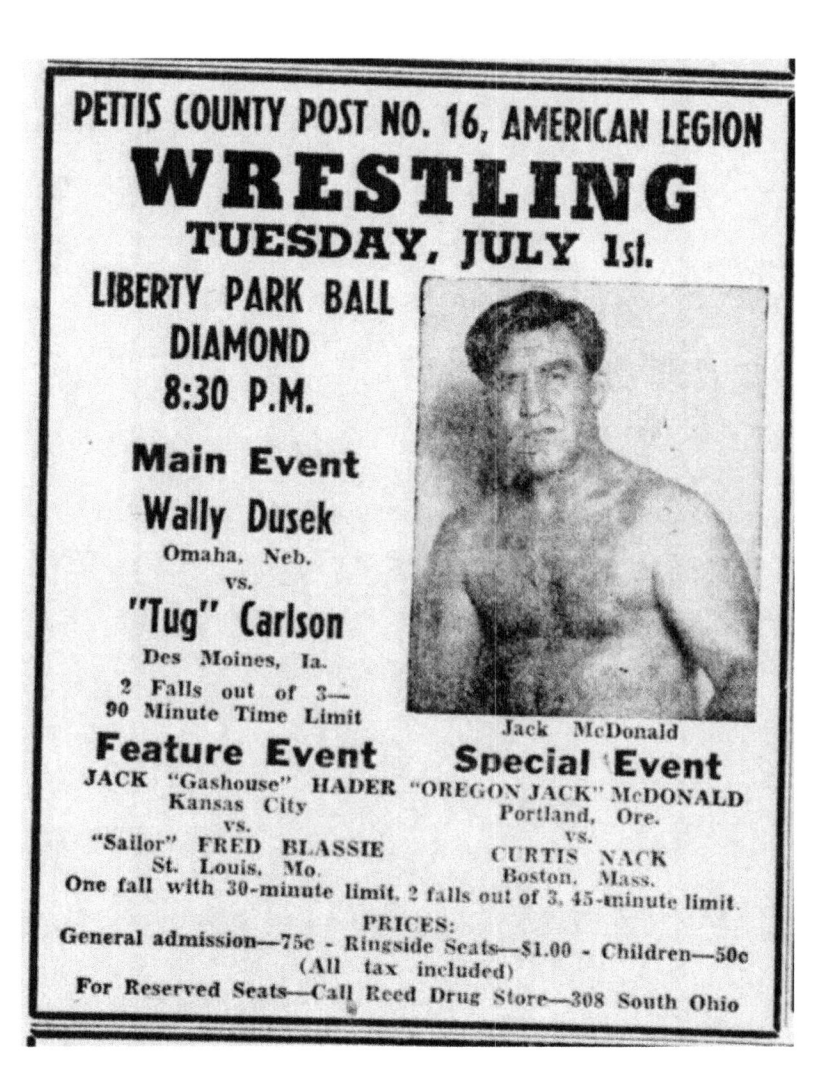

1947 card in Sedalia, Missouri.

NO TIME LIMIT.

WRESTLING TONIGHT ARMORY

8:30 P. M.

JIM WRIGHT
VS.
TUG CARLSON

RONNIE ETCHISON
VS.
TONY SANATRA

REX MAYES
VS.
WALTER ACTHU

REFEREE, DICK PATTON.
TICKETS ON SALE AT SARATOGA CAFE, MECCA CAFE, RUST BROS., SNACK SHOP.

50c—$1.00—$1.50
Tax Included.
GEO HILLS, Promoter.

1949 card in Terre Haute, Indiana.

TUG CARLSON.

One of the last times Tug Carlson appeared in a newspaper, 1949.

Above: Louisville, Kentucky ad, May of 1949. Below: The night Tug Carlson tagged with Gorgeous George. (Nagurski was a no-show.)

TUG CARLSON.

Another photo from his final year as Carlson.

Wilbur Finran, the Ohio farm boy who became Lord Patrick Lansdowne of the House of Barrington.

HEIRS OF LORD LANSDOWNE

In the wrestling business, the goal of every great heel is to generate heat (wrestler speak for getting the audience to genuinely hate you). There are some cheap, quick ways to get heat for a night, such as wearing a Red Sox hat in Madison Square Garden, but true heat comes from creating a character that the people hate with every fiber of their being. Heels like this are almost extinct in today's wrestling, but in the 1950s, wrestlers who were willing to be hated could become very rich men.

Wrestlers have long been able to call on nationalism and xenophobia to create long lasting heel characters. If you were an Asian wrestler the 1940s and wanted to become a star, you made yourself Japanese. It didn't matter if you were Chinese, Samoan, Filipino, or third generation American, if you looked Asian, you chose a Japanese name and became public enemy number one.

German and Italian characters were instant heat seekers as well. During the war years it looked as if the Germans were invading America by way of the squared circle. German heels continued to pop up for decades to come including Fritz Von Erich (a good ol' boy from Texas) and Baron von Raschke (a real life Nebraska farm boy).

Even before German heels went out of fashion, the Russians began to supplant them as the heels-to-be for Caucasian stars. The Volkoffs, the Koloffs, the

Kalmikoffs, Boris Zhukov, and Khrusher Khruschev were but a few of the red menaces to invade America in the late 20th Century.

The United States continued to feel the heat from the Pacific as Mr. Fuji brought wave after wave of Japanese wrestlers to the WWF in the 80s and 90s. And let's not forget the Arabs! Real life Middle Eastern warriors like the Iron Sheik and phony Arabs like the original Sheik all struck terror in the hearts of wrestling fans.

A foreign language, a foreign flag, and keen awareness of current events helped a lot of wrestlers get over with foreign gimmicks. Yet while Germans and Russians and Arabs have come and gone over the years, one unlikely nation has always had the uncanny ability to create stars Americans hate: Great Britain.

It's hard to put a finger on why the British draw so much ire from American wrestling fans. True, we did fight two wars with them for our independence, but that was over two centuries ago. All those who were there to witness the cruelty of King George and other monarchs are long dead, as are King George and his contemporaries. We buried the hatchet in the 19th century and became allies in two World Wars. We co-founded the League of Nations and the United Nations. We're buddies. We're pals. Right?

Strange as it seems, after all this time, there's something about the British that turn us off. Maybe it's the way the British wrestlers put on airs. Maybe it's their music. Maybe it's the robes that remind us royalty and the oppression our great-great-great-great-great-great-great grandparents suffered. Maybe it's the accent, the high and mighty way they speak our language that always sounds like they are talking down to us.

This leads us back to the 1930s and a wrestler by the name of Wilbur Finran. Finran was born far from the Cliffs of Dover in Springfield, Ohio back in 1905. He was an athlete from the start participating in gymnastics, swimming, and wrestling at the YMCA while only a boy. He made his debut in the late 1920s working for legendary promoter Al Haft. He was not a big man, barely 175 pounds, but he had a fertile imagination that would serve him well.

Haft turned Finran into Pat "Duke" Finnegan, giving him an Irish-American persona to appeal to the Irish population in Columbus. Finran continued to evolve the character, transforming from "Duke" to "Lord" Finnegan and eventually to Lord Patrick Lansdowne from the fictitious House of Barrington. Such name changes were easily handled in the days before television and the Internet, but when Braven Dyer of the *Los Angeles Times* asked about the name change, Lansdowne was ready with an answer. His real name, he claimed, was "too weighty" for simple Midwesterners. "This arose because of my last name, which caused some of the writers a great deal of trouble. I never bothered about correcting them when they billed me as Lord Finnegan."

The man from the House of Barrington was responsible for a number of innovations in professional wrestling. When a band was available, he would have them play "God Save the Queen," becoming the first wrestler to use an entrance theme. He wore a monocle, a purple robe, and a black tunic to the ring that allegedly were valued at over $2000.

Lansdowne also employed several valets and was accompanied by one or two at his matches. His aides bore names like Tweedles, Twittles, and Jeeves. They assisted their master with his robes, and if they were careless with them, his Lordship would step out of the ring to show them how to properly fold his garments.

Lansdowne's valets would use an atomizer supposedly filled with perfume to disinfect the ring, a gimmick that Gorgeous George would borrow with his own brand of perfume. In between falls, the valets would bring tea service for their master, a simple act that only served to further rile the American fans.

Lansdowne also invented "the stall," the art of delaying the match with outrageous antics that only serve to enrage the fans and generate more heat. While wrestling in Louisville during 1938, Lansdowne held his hand up just after the bell rang, asking for a moment to prepare. He then went into an elaborate routine of stretching and exercising, an act that drove the fans into a frenzy. They hated his lordship with a passion - so much so that the promotion was sold out for the next eight weeks.

Lord Lansdowne became that rare gimmick that had an opposite effect on male and female fans. His British manner and haughtiness had men calling for his head while the women (many of them wives of the same men who wanted Lansdowne murdered) lined the barrier on the way back to the locker room, hoping to get an autograph or at least catch the eye of the handsome Brit. Some nights it took him more than 30 minutes to get to the back for all the autograph seekers.

Becoming Lord Lansdowne made Wilbur Finran a sensation, especially on the West Coast. He became friends with the rich and the famous, and he was especially popular with the movie star set. He also found himself connected with two high profile murder investigations, including the death of actress Thelma Todd in December of 1935. Lansdowne was one of the last people to speak to Todd prior to her death by carbon monoxide poisoning in her own garage and was called in to testify. Although the death was ruled an accident, it remains a subject of mystery to this day.

Lansdowne was truly the first in a new wave of character wrestlers that would revolutionize the sport of professional wrestling. Sadly, his career came to a screeching halt in the early 1950s when he was diagnosed with Lou Gehrig's disease. The disease took it's slow, painful toll on the former star, and in 1959, he died in Columbus, Ohio.

The fact that Lansdowne is little remembered today is a testimony to the incredible influence he had on professional wrestling. He was, as the *Columbus Evening Dispatch* stated upon his death, the original glamour wrestler, but his legacy faded into the shadows, obscured by those who followed the trail he blazed.

George Wagner was the first to adapt the Lord Lansdowne act and make it his own, but rather than take up the British mantle, Wagner took the pomp and pageantry of Lansdowne to the extreme. He grew out his dark hair and dyed it a shocking blonde color. He called on legendary stylists Frank and Joseph of Hollywood to create a hairstyle uniquely his own, the Marcel. He changed his black tights to lilac and commissioned a series of flowing, effeminate robes to wear to the ring. He swapped "God Save the Queen" for "Pomp and Circumstance," and he hired on a valet who would spray the ring down with his own fragrance, Chanel No. 10.

"Why not Chanel No. 5?" asked ring announcers everywhere.

"Why be half safe?" George would reply.

Gorgeous George came along at the right time in wrestling history. He was a star made for the camera, and the television audiences loved him. The Gorgeous One made appearances on numerous television programs and, like Lansdowne before him, became popular with the Hollywood crowd. He even appeared in a motion picture, *Alias the Champ*, a B-reel murder mystery that was more or less an excuse to cash in on the enormous popularity of its star.

The accidental tag match in 1948 wasn't the first time Tug Carlson appeared on a bill with Gorgeous George, but it was his first recorded appearance in the ring with the man they called the Human Orchid. Like everyone else, my father saw dollar signs when he saw the Gorgeous George act.

While it would be easy to say my father borrowed from Gorgeous George, the truth is my father is just as much a son of Lord Lansdowne as the Gorgeous One. The former chose to accentuate the glamorous side of the House of Barrington, creating an act unequaled in his day for glitz, glamour, and over the top outrageousness. Leo Whippern took a different route, following in the footsteps of the phony Brit to create his own despicable nobleman.

GORGEOUS GEORGE AND HIS VALET JEFFERY

The eldest of Lord Lansdowne's "heirs," Gorgeous George and his valet Jeffrey.

GORGEOUS AT THE GREAT HOLLYWOOD BENEFIT

Rare photo of Gorgeous George at a Hollywood Benefit. Burt Lancaster was his opponent. Bob Hope took on the role of Jeffrey.

Lord Carlton had his share of celebrity admirers. I'm told that Faye Emerson was quite taken with him!

Action shot of Lord Carlton from my photo collection.

HIS LORDSHIP ARRIVES

It's not at all uncommon for people in entertainment to reinvent themselves in order to prolong their careers. As actors age, the roles they take on change. Musicians change with the times, following trends and experimenting with new technology. Wrestlers are no different. My father wasn't the first and he certainly wasn't the last to change his persona in order to extend his career. Hulk Hogan, the Undertaker, and Mick Foley are modern examples of men who saw an opportunity to change their persona and extended their careers.

My father's change, however, was more like Mick Foley's than Hogan and Undertaker. While the latter two merely became different incarnations of the same core character, Foley changed from Cactus Jack to Mankind to Dude Love, and back again. He remains the only WWE Superstar to appear as three different people in the same Royal Rumble.

Tug Carlson had worked both babyface and heel. He knew how to play the darling hero of the people, and he knew how to play dirty. He was particularly known for using the tape on his hands to scrape off the skin of babyface opponents. Many wrestlers will tell you it's more fun to be bad than good, and Tug Carlson was one of the best in his day. But Leo Whippern was offered an opportunity to become a bigger heel and a bigger draw by changing his persona completely.

In a 1952 interview, Pedro Martinez admitted that Lord Carlton was the former Tug Carlson. Martinez ran the Manhattan booking office for legendary promoter Toots Mondt. "His real name is Leo Whippern and he came from San Francisco. He used to wrestle under the name of Tug Carlson of the U.S. Navy. We thought up the gimmick of the monocle and valet. All he has to do is work in the ring. We do the rest."

Leo always grew up believing he was royalty. He was very in touch with his royal roots thanks to conversations he supposedly had with his grandfather, Baron Bernhardt Herzbrun, so it was perfectly natural for my father to embrace those royal roots through his in-ring persona. But why did he choose to become nobleman of English heritage instead of the more provable Austrian?

My brother Kitt says he asked Leo that very question and received a very practical answer.

""Are you insane? My professional wrestling career started just after WWII. Had I portrayed Austrian nobility, the 'fans' would not have simply booed or hissed at me, they would have come to the arena with guns and killed me. They would have at least had the FBI show up and tried to have me deported back to the Nuremberg Trials in Germany."

In May of 1949, Tug Carlson bid farewell to the United States, wrestling his final match on American soil against Wee Willie Davis in Buffalo, New York on May 20. He headed north of the border to do a series of matches in Toronto for Maple Leaf Wrestling, culminating with a loss to African-American star Seelie Samara on September 22. That would be the final time Tug Carlson would ever set foot in the ring.

On October 8, 1949 at the Broadway Arena in New York City, the British nobleman made his debut on American soil. He wore a splendid robe and looked down on the unwashed masses through a monocle. Lord Leslie Carlton, as he was now known, had come to America to demonstrate his immense knowledge and skill of the grappling game.

Fact mingled with fiction as my father crafted a completely new identity in the ring. Wrestling publications made mention of the illness my father had as a child, but the setting was no longer America, but Ipswitch, England, where my father was raised with courtly manners fitting of a noble birth. He was said to have been a graduate of Jesus College at Oxford University where he participated in cricket, tumbling, boxing, and of course wrestling.

Like Leo Whippern, Lord Carlton went to see as a young man, enlisting in the British Naval Academy in 1939 at the outbreak of war. He was transferred to the Royal Navy and assigned to the East Asia Command under Lord Louis Mountbatten at Calcutta.

It was in Calcutta that Lord Carlton was first introduced to professional wrestling. Having bested all the top grapplers in the Royal Navy, a match was arranged between the British noble and Mohamed Ali, student of India's greatest wrestling champion Gama. Lord Carlton was too much for Ali, who praised the foreigner at the completion of their match, and all agreed his success was an omen of things to come.

Now crowned champion of the Royal Navy and India, Lord Carlton next took on the Egyptian champion Harmeda and Scottish champion Cpl. George Shank, scoring victories over both men.

It was only after this victory that Carlton began considering a career in professional wrestling, but when he returned home after the war, he was forced to do so incognito, so as to not bring disgrace on his noble birth. He was said to have wrestled under an alias in Europe, racking up one victory after another. Then one night, a distant relative was at ringside to witness Carlton's greatness. He urged the promising young athlete to do away with the alias, to bear his royal title in the ring, and make his country proud.

Quite a story, isn't it?

Like Lord Lansdowne before him, Lord Carlton brought along a second to attend to him at ringside. The earliest valet was known as Sir James Hartley, an English butler dressed in a Prince Albert coat, purple cummerbund, and a monocle, was the very model of a British servant. In other matches Carlton was accompanied by Leftenant Malcolm (or James) Waite, who carried a cane to the ring that was used to signal his charge and, when needed, deliver a low blow behind the official's back. The valet's presence only added more fuel to the fire when Carlton took to the ring.

My father was extremely athletic in the ring. He could flip and tumble with ease. He could reverse out of an arm bar with a standing back flip. He was quick and he was agile. Becoming Lord Carlton added a new dimension to the athletic ring work. Lord Carlton was meaner than Tug Carlson on his worst day. He played dirty every chance he got, taking cheap shots, using the ropes, and jabbing a quick finger in his opponent's eye. Outside the ring, he sipped tea during interviews and sneered at the people with a haughty eye. The meaner he was, the more fans hated him, and the more they hated him, the more money he drew.

Lord Carlton's quick ascent to the top was helped in part by a new medium bringing wrestling to the masses. Television was beginning to make inroads across the United States, and fledgling televisions stations, eager for content, found an inexpensive cash cow in professional wrestling. Unlike outdoor sports like football and baseball, wrestling was fairly easy and inexpensive to shoot. Promoters were a bit leery of the medium at first, fearing that fans would watch from home and skip the live shows. However, once the new generation of colorful characters like Lord Carlton began appearing on their black and white screens, viewer ratings and box office takes began to soar.

Six months into his new life as a British nobleman, Lord Carlton headlined the world's most famous arena, Madison Square Garden, with the biggest star in the world. His name was Antonino Rocca, and he was an immigrant from Italy by way of Argentina. A natural athlete, Rocca excelled at both soccer and rugby in his younger years, but he began training to become a wrestler in Argentina under former world champion Stanislaus Zbyszko.

Toots Mondt put Rocca under exclusive contract in 1949, and Rocca became the poster boy for the New York promotion, reviving wrestling in a city that had been largely dead since the mid 1930s. Rocca and Mondt were laying the ground work for what would become Capital Wrestling, the predecessor of the World Wide Wrestling Federation that eventually became the WWE.

It took a great heel to make the fans get behind a great babyface, and in May of 1950, that role fell to Lord Carlton. 14,246 fans packed the Gardens on May 15, 1950, and the promoters brought in a total of $43,311 at the gate, an astonishing figure especially in that day. Fans were thrilled when the heinous Lord Carlton lost two out of three falls to Rocca that night.

Although Rocca was a huge star, my father didn't think much of him as a true wrestler. Rocca was all show, but my father came from an era when wrestlers knew how to shoot (wrestler speak for legitimate wrestling, often used to settle disputes or prove point). According to Johnny Andriolo, he grew weary of making Rocca look good.

"Tug had a series of matches with Rocca that went to a draw. One night after a match, he went to the promoter and said, 'I'm going to beat him the next time we wrestle.' They didn't want Tug to beat their star, so they paid him thousands of dollars just to leave!"

In the spring of 1951 Carlton came face to face with another English nobleman, Lord Blears. Blears was one of the few English gentlemen who was actually English. Not only that, he was a war hero with quite a tale. When his ship was sunk by a Japanese submarine, he and a handful of other survivors were pulled on board by the Japanese, who tied their wrists and took them away a few at a time to be executed.

Blears heard the gun shots from afar and managed to keep his wrists loose in the binding. When the Japanese sailors came for him, Blears struck first, knocking his captors away and dragging a fellow sailor into the water. The other sailor died in the escape attempt, but Blears, an Olympic caliber swimmer, managed to swim out of range of machine gun fire and stay afloat long enough to be rescued by an American naval vessel.

If any man had reason to have a beef with my father, it was Blears, who was everything my father pretended to be and then some. He called Lord Carlton a "bounder" and an "imposter," and a feud ignited in New York.

Blears had a second of his own, Captain Leslie Holmes, to protect him from any malfeasance from Lt. Waite when the two met on March 13, 1951. He also had a retriever named Bruce and brought with him "official" Lord Blears monocles that he would hand out to fans.

A crowd of 1400 fans was on hand in Syracuse for the confrontation between the two English gentlemen. When the monocles came off and the battle began, it was Blears who would score the first pin fall 27 minutes into the match. Referee Jack Millicich made what Carlton felt was a fast three count, and he flew into a rage. Carlton attacked Captain Holmes, tossing him from the ring, and then turned to slam the referee. His caustic actions cost him a penalty fall, and the real British nobleman, Blears, left with a controversial two falls to none victory.

Despite the occasional high profile losses, Lord Carlton's stock continued to soar. He traveled to New Jersey, Maryland, and Washington D.C. He did battle with old, familiar faces like the Duseks and Babe Zaharias and new stars like Golden Superman, Arnold Skaaland, and "Mr. America" Gene Stanlee. Carlton racked up an impressive series of wins, as any good heel should, and remained a top draw into mid 1951.

A wrestler never stayed too long in one place, and His Lordship was only beginning his conquest of the former colonies. Lord Carlton's next stop would be one unfamiliar to him yet very familiar to the man who bore his name. He would travel to California, now the center of the televised wrestling universe, before heading out to conquer the rest of the states.

Lord Leslie Carlton and valet.

Lord Carlton takes to the air against Antonino Rocca.

Lord Leslie Carlton at home with my Mom and my brother.

Above: Lord Carlton and the Swami. The robe in this photo is one of the few in my collection. Below: Lt. James Waite assisting my father.

84

THE SWAMI

Anyone who remembers wrestling in the 80s can't think about Randy Savage without thinking about his constant companion, Miss Elizabeth. When Randy made his grand entrance in his sequined robe and over-sized shades to "Pomp and Circumstance," he had a beautiful woman by his side every step of the way. Fans who hated Randy when he was a heel adored Elizabeth and wondered what such a sweet woman could be doing with such a despicable heel. They booed Randy when he cast her aside in his rivalry with Hulk Hogan, and they cheered when the two were reunited and later married, right in the wrestling ring.

None of this was new, of course. Every bit of the Randy and Miss Elizabeth story had already been done, going way back to the 1920s. Before he took on the Gorgeous persona, George Wagner married his first wife Betty in the ring in 1939. The wedding was such a huge draw they got married again and again all over the country.

Betty also acted as Gorgeous George's valet in the early days, escorting him to the ring and assisting with his robes. She was followed by a number of male assistants who took on the part of George's valet Jeffrey. Bob Hope even took on the part one evening when George wrestled a charity match against Burt Lancaster.

Of course Gorgeous George was not the first to have a valet escort him to the ring. Lord Patrick Lansdowne and his faithful man servants were the inspiration for Jeffrey as well as Sir James and Leftenant Waite. But when Lord Carlton returned to the West Coast, he took the act one step further when he teamed up with the Swami.

The idea for the Swami was a natural extension of Lord Leslie Carlton's legend. Being that Lord Carlton began wrestling when he served in Her Majesty's armed forces in India, it seemed fitting that his lordship would pick up a mystical Swami to act as his valet.

My cousin's father Frank Romano was the first man to play the Swami character, also known as Jelil Singh. It's possible Frank Romano's service to his country - the United States, that is - inspired the origin of the Swami. Frank served in the U.S. Army during World War II and traveled to both Burma and India, working on the Burma Road, the Lido Road and the Stillwell Road. Romano had worked as a dancer prior to the war, and after the war, he married my aunt. Through my aunt, my father and Frank became friends and created the character that would act as Lord Carlton's assistant and advisor.

The Swami made his debut in August of 1952. In many ways the Swami became more active at ringside than Gorgeous George's Jeffrey. He assisted his lordship with his robes, but when the match began, he kept a close eye on his charge. He would hop up on the ring apron and shout instructions to Lord Carlton, much like managers Jim Cornette and "Classy" Freddie Blassie in later years. The implication was that Lord Carlton was relying not only on the Swami's knowledge of combat, but ancient Hindu wisdom.

His usual wardrobe was a tuxedo with a white turban adorned with a large jewel, a magical gem believed to have mystical powers. Some sports reporters claimed that the Swami would use the jewel to cast spells on Lord Carlton's opponents.

Frank Romano would pass the role of the Swami off to a former wrestler named Tommy Peratis, a Greek who used to tag with Frank Jares, better known as The Thing. As the Swami, Peratis would babble instructions to Lord Carlton throughout his matches. The noise inside the arenas was too loud for anyone to realize that Peratis was actually speaking Greek and not Hindi.

Fans were never sure whether the Swami was a legitimate practitioner of the mystical arts or a sham. He put on a good show both as advisor to Carlton and potential jinx to the babyface, but more often than not, the crooked Swami resorted to old fashioned dirty tricks to guarantee a victory. Like all ringside companions the Swami was adept at distracting referee, passing a concealed weapon to his charge, and when all else fails - tripping a babyface as he bounces off the ropes.

Just like Jeffrey and George, Lord Carlton and his sidekicks were indelibly tied together in the minds of the fans. This was the age of kayfabe, where what happened in the ring was purportedly 100% real. It was on my father and the other wrestlers to keep up appearances twenty-four hours a day, seven days a week.

There's an amusing anecdote that further illustrates my father's connection to the Swami in Chad Dell's book *The Revenge of Hatpin Mary: Women, Professional Wrestling, and Fan Culture in the 1950s.*

Dell tells the story of a Chicago newspaper writer who wrote a column titled "Chit Chat... by Ann." The columnist was on her way to the matches one night. She boarded the "El" train and was surprised to see none other than Lord Carlton stepping on board the train, alone, carrying his own bags.

"Ann," as she called herself, was a left-leaning writer, who was not yet over the 1952 election of Dwight D. Eisenhower to the White House. Eisenhower was the first Republican since Herbert Hoover to ascend to the nation's highest office, and like many Democrats of the day, she genuinely feared that a Republican administration would mean a quick return to the the dark days of unemployment and bread lines.

When Ann saw the Lord Carlton on board the train, bearing his own luggages, it sent chills down her spine. Lord Carton, after all was royalty. He was one of the "haves" of society, and it was expected that away from the ring, Lord Carlton's faithful Swami would be by his side bearing his luggage.

Where was the Swami? Why was Lord Leslie Carlton riding the train to the matches and not the limousine? Ann was certain her worst fears about the new president were already coming true!

Ann stepped off the train at the same stop as my father. Heading in the same direction, they struck up a conversation on their way to the Arena. Ann just had to know if Carlton's current travel situation was a sign of the times, so as they walked the Chicago streets, she confessed her fears about the recent election and her worries that my father might already be feeling the effects of the Eisenhower administration.

Lord Carlton took it all with grace and humor, and he assured the lady he was doing just fine. His swami and his fancy car, he said, were both in Georgia, and he would be reunited with them soon. Ann was satisfied with his answer, assured the second Great Depression was not already underway.

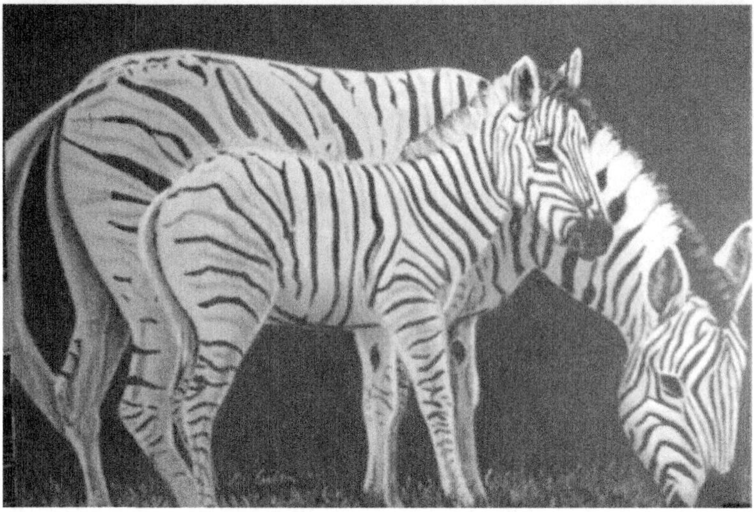

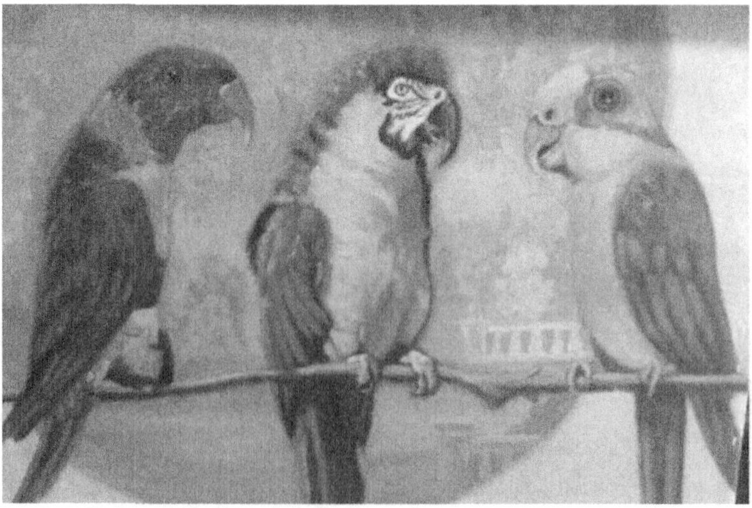

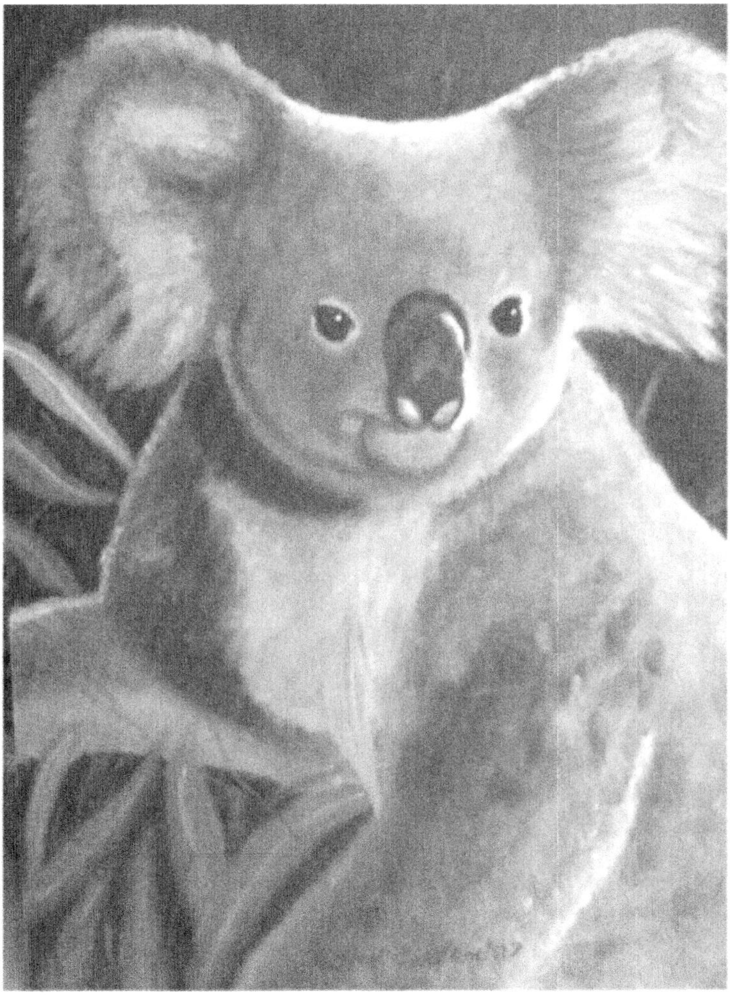

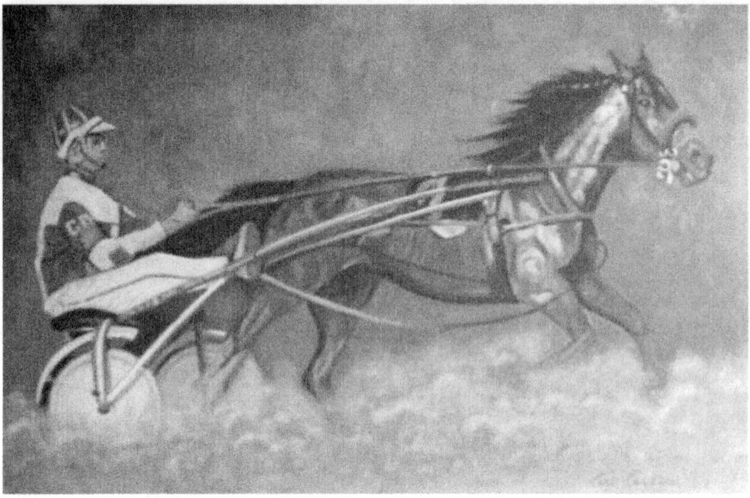

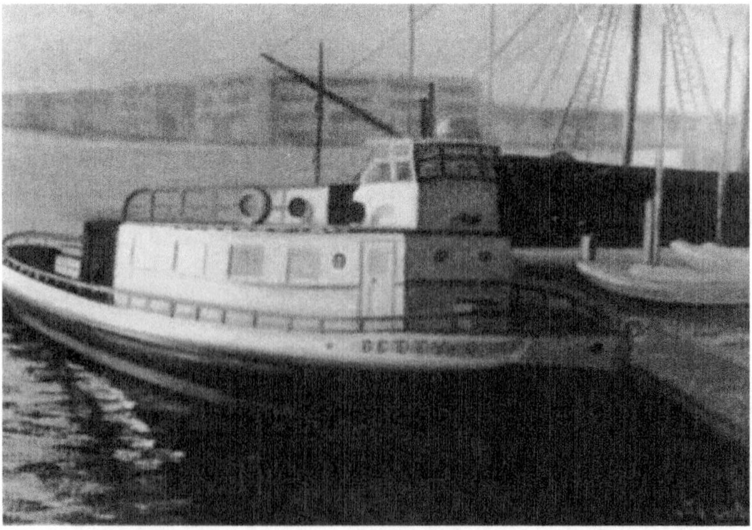

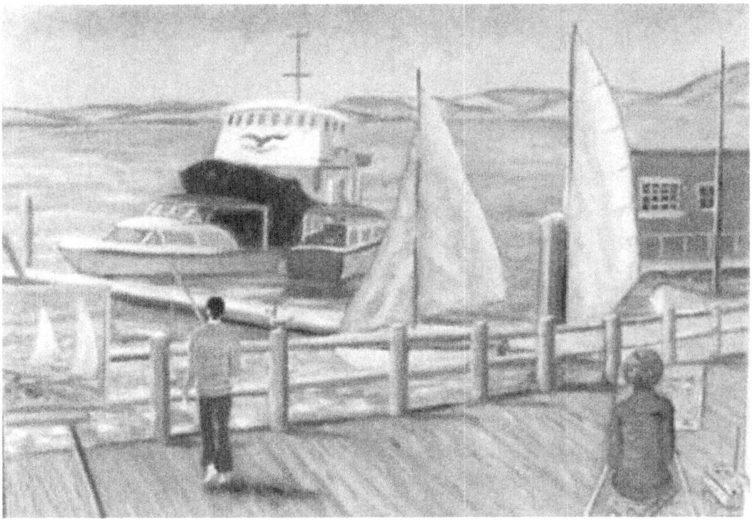

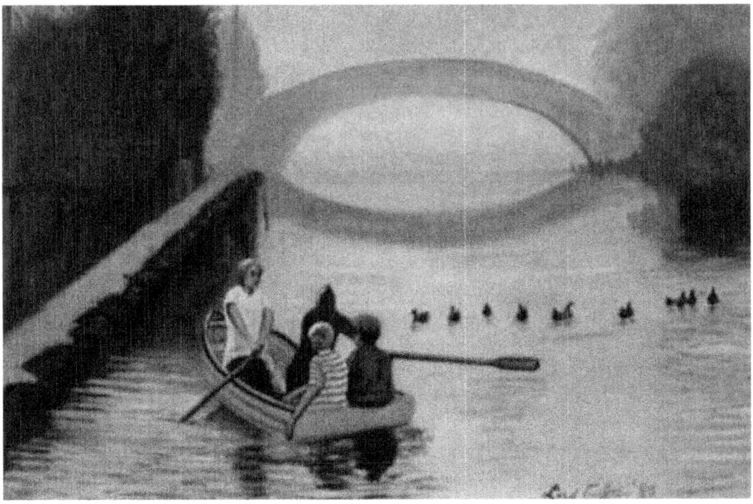

On the cover of *Boxing and Wrestling* 1952.

CONQUERING THE STATES

When Lord Leslie Carlton and the Swami arrived on the West Coast, they took the new territory by storm much as they had the East. Los Angeles was now one of the hottest wrestling towns in America, and *Wrestling from Hollywood* on the ABC television network, broadcast from the legendary Olympic Auditorium, was one of the biggest TV shows in the country. LA booker Johnny Doyle claimed the audience for the Hollywood wrestling show to be ten times as much as the audience for baseball.

Carlton established himself as a heel and a force to be reckoned with. He scored wins over Sam Menacker, Pat Fraley, Pat McGill, Enrique Torres, and Chief Lone Eagle. In December and into early 1952, he expanded his travels to include Arizona, Utah, New Mexico, and Western Texas, continuing his dirty, winning ways.

Whether it was his own creativity or the wisdom of the Swami, Lord Carlton was expanding his repertoire, finding new ways to cheat to win. An El Paso paper from early 1952 describes Carlton as using an under the ring "surprise attack" to steal a victory from rival Juan Renesto, better known as Tom Renesto.

In February Carlton headed back east. He dove right into a marquee match up with one of the biggest East Coast stars of the early 1950s, Gene Stanlee.

Known as "Mr. America," Stanlee's life story was remarkably similar to my father. He was born in Chicago to Polish immigrants, and as a young boy, he was partially paralyzed after taking a tumble down stairs. He was given last rites, but after seeing a strong man perform at his church, he was inspired. The young man recovered and dedicated himself to the sport of body building. He served in the Navy during World War II, and in 1946 he took up the sport of professional wrestling. Carlton defeated Mr. America twice in February of 1952, once in Jamaica, New York, and once in Washington, D.C.

Lord Carlton played dirty inside and outside the ring. By chance or by choice, sometimes fans got in the way, and an incident that took place in the crowd while working for Toots Mondt would send my father into a much different arena.

In March of 1952 Carlton was sued by a fan named Emma Talmadge, in Baltimore, Maryland. The 122 pound Talmadge filed a personal injury suit against the 220-pound wrestler. The $10,000 lawsuit claimed that Talmadge required medical treatment after Carlton smacked her while navigating a hostile Baltimore Coliseum crowd.

Talmadge hired a lawyer who took full advantage of the suit to try and earn himself some fame and glory. Hyman Pressman took out a newspaper ad challenging Lord Carlton to a wrestling match under AAU rules to "prove Lord Leslie Carlton is a big bum." Carlton responded, "Anytime, anywhere," but the match never took place.

The courtroom battle did, and Carlton was as quick with the judge as he was with his opponents in defending his innocence.

"I was flanked fore and aft by ushers," Carlton said, insisting he could not possibly have slapped the woman. "Perhaps this is a case of racial discrimination because I'm British."

The judge asked Lord Carlton whether he was in fact a Lord or even British. My father turned up his nose and replied, "That question is irrelevant, immaterial, and has no bearing on this case," he maintained.

"Well, you were a detestable villain that night, weren't you?" Pressman said.

"Detestable?" said Lord Carlton. "In my opinion, I'm not detestable."

Pressman had a lot of flair and flamboyance. He might have made a great promoter or manager in another life. But on that day, he was beaten on his home turf. The judge acquitted Lord Carlton of all charges in only 97 minutes. Lord Carlton fought the law, and the law was counted out. If winning in the squared circle made the fans angry, my father knew that winning in the court of American law would make them hate his British alter ego even more!

"He played the part of the villain all day every day," says Karl Lauer, former president of the Cauliflower Alley Club. Lauer grew up on the West Coast and remembers Lord Carlton well. "He was sort of a loner in the locker room, but he was always warm and friendly. That changed the moment people who were not in the business walked in the room. He looked down his nose at everyone through that monocle. And he never signed an autograph that I know of. I've seen some that are supposedly his, but my guess is most if not all are fakes. Heels didn't sign autographs, and Lord Carlton would not sign for anyone!"

Lord Carlton headed to the Southwestern territory, El Paso to Arizona, to meet some old foes and new. Jack Claybourne was another African-American pioneer, one of the first to work against high profile white wrestlers. My father wrestled two Broadways (wrestler speak for a time limit draw) against the world traveler Claybourne and several tag matches. Claybourne was once known as "Gentleman" Jack Claybourne but was working under the name Black Panther, a moniker originated by his sometime rival Jim Mitchell.

Dory Funk was a Hoosier from Hammond, Indiana who served in the Navy during World War II. He later relocated to Amarillo, Texas, where he would become a promoter. He also fathered two of the greatest legends in the business, Dory, Jr. and Terry Funk. Both men went on to be tag champions and world champions.

Another rising star who crossed paths with Lord Carlton was Mexican star Gory Guerrero. Guerrero was one of the top stars in the early days of Lucha Libre and, like Funk, became patriarch of one of the greatest wrestling families in history. His sons Chavo, Mando, Hector, and Eddie all followed him into the business. Eddie and nephew Chavo, Jr., went on to greater fame in WCW and WWE.

The biggest star Lord Carlton would face that summer was an immigrant from Italy who, like my father, got his start as a boxer. That shared past would play a major factor in their feud during the summer of 1952.

Primo Carrera was an Italian immigrant billed as the tallest wrestler in America. Carnera was 6' 5 1/2", but he was billed as 6' 7". He was discovered by a traveling circus in 1925 and hired on as a wrestler. Carnera also took up boxing, and, was undefeated in his home country, thanks in no small part to some crooked promoters who arranged victories for the rising star.

Carnera emigrated to the United States in 1930. These were the days of prohibition, and the Italian-American mafia took a keen interest in the young boxer. When Carnera discovered his manager was channeling his winnings back to the mob, Carnera broke ties with him and returned to Italy. He came back to the States with new management and his eyes set on the world heavyweight championship.

Carnera became the first Italian-American to win the heavyweight boxing title when he defeated Jack Sharkey at Madison Square Garden in 1933. A year later he dropped the belt to the smaller but more experienced Max Baer, father of *Beverly Hillbillies* star Max Baer, Jr.

Carnera's boxing career took a downturn after the loss to Baer. He found himself working lower card matches with lesser names when his health allowed him to fight. He finally hung up the gloves in 1946 and returned to wrestling just as the business was hitting a new boom period. He was in the right place at the right time, and Carnera became a rising star.

Carnera and Lord Carlton traded wins on several occasions in the summer of 1952. During a match in mid-July match in Albuquerque, Lord Carlton stole a fall when the Swami reached into the ring and tripped Carnera, allowing Lord Carlton to drop on top and steal a quick pin. Fans protested the dirty deed loudly, but the referee, suffered the same blindness most wrestling refs do and never saw the Swami. Security had to sweep the ref, the Swami, and the victor to the safety of the locker room, and it was several minutes before order was restored and the night's action could resume.

A rematch was set for the end of July, and this time two referees were promised to keep my father and the Swami from cheating. According to the *Albuquerque Journal*, Lord Carlton was unable to wrestle the rematch due to a throat injury, and Carnera faced Jesus Ortega instead.

When Lord Carlton won by count out in Tucson a few nights later, Carnera had enough. He went after Lord Carlton and gave him a good beating after the bell had sounded, setting the stage for what would turn out to be a boxing match to settle the score between the two.

News that Primo Carnera was going to box again after six years made this a must-see main event. More than 5000 people packed into Hi Corbett Field in Tucson for a ten round affair between the arch rivals.

My father knew how to work a pair of gloves, but this time, it was the towering former champion who got the win. Lord Carlton lost by a knockout in the third round to the delight of the crowd, putting an exclamation point on a thrilling summer rivalry.

Gene Stanlee, "Mr. America," in a photo ad from Pennsylvania.

Lord Carlton in a fan magazine from the early 1950s.
Photo courtesy Jim Oetkins.

Photo ad for the boxing match against Primo Carnera in Tucson.

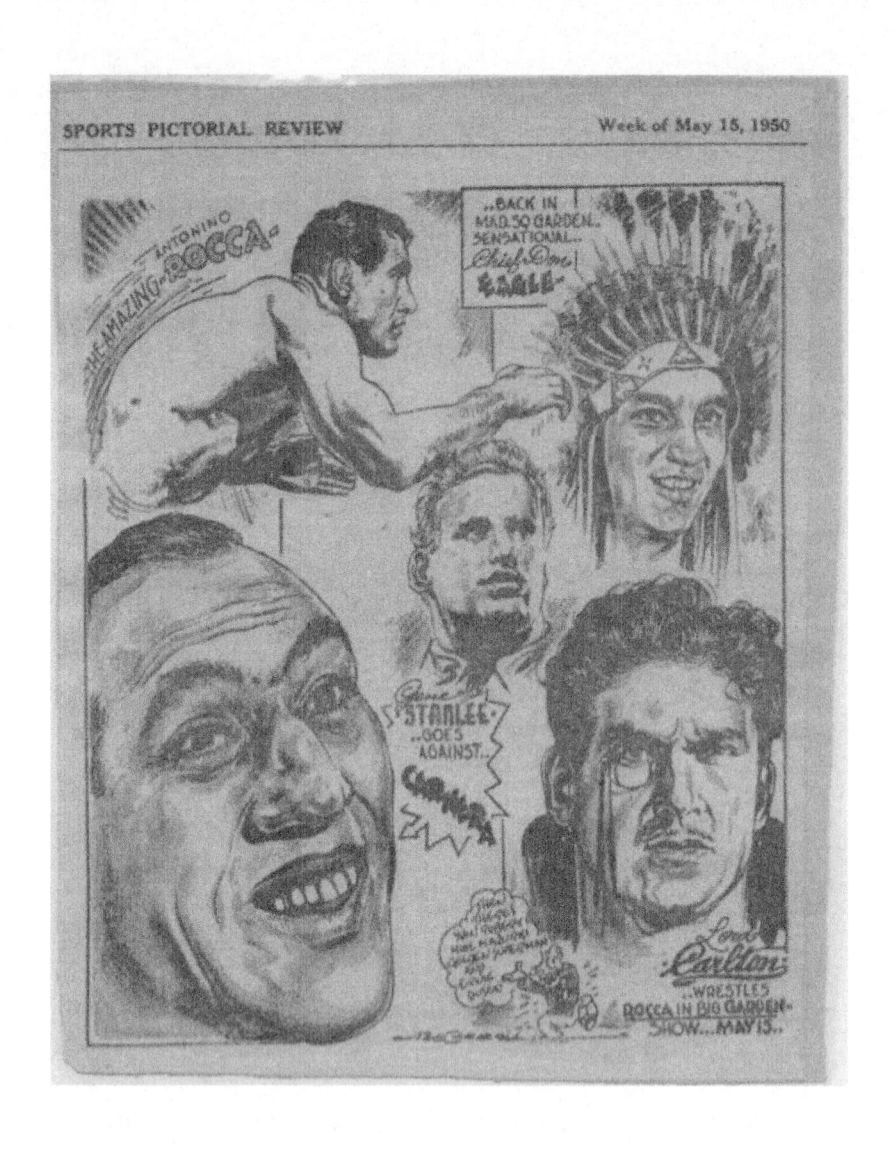

Cartoon featuring Antonino Rocca, Don Eagle, Gene Stanlee, Primo Carnera, and Lord Leslie Carlton.

Postcard from Dad's good friend, Freddie Blassie.

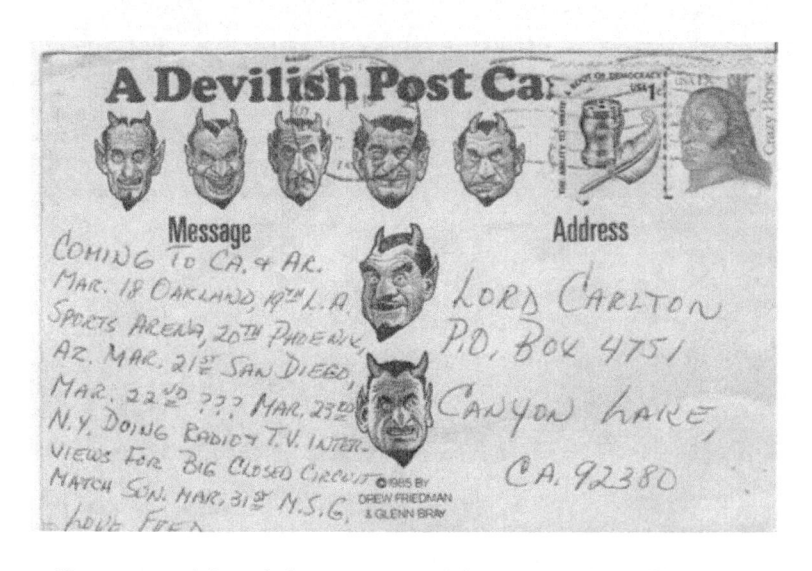

Reverse side of the postcard from Freddie Blassie.

FAMOUS FRIENDS

The WWE has worked hard to present its top superstars not simply as wrestling stars but mainstream celebrities. When Vince McMahon took his father's company national in the 1980s, Hulk Hogan became a household name. Hulk made movies, appeared on TV shows like *The A-Team*, and even had his own Saturday morning cartoon.

Andre the Giant was already a huge star when he made *The Princess Bride*, but that movie made him a legend. Since then countless WWE stars have found success outside of wrestling, including Roddy Piper, The Rock, Steve Austin, and John Cena.

The marketing machine behind WWE had a lot to do with their success, but the celebrity status they attained was really nothing new. Back in the 1950s all it took was the explosion of TV sales and a program called *Wrestling from Hollywood* to make many wrestlers, including Lord Leslie Carlton, into household names.

Gorgeous George was the breakout star of the group. In fact when television writers look back at that era, Gorgeous George is often considered the number two television star of his day, second only to Milton Berle. He appeared on numerous talk and variety shows and took full advantage of the new medium.

My father didn't have quite the success beyond wrestling that Gorgeous George did, but he did make an appearance on the game show *To Tell The Truth*.

The show featured three people who all claimed to be a person with an unusual job or background. Two of the men/women were imposters, but the third was sworn to tell the truth about themselves. A panel of four celebrity contestants would try to guess which of the three was the real deal.

Lord Carlton made some famous friends in his day, and a number of those friendships lasted for life. One of the few wrestlers he kept in touch with long after his days in the ring ended was another former sailor, "Classy" Freddie Blassie. Blassie was inspired to dye his locks blonde by Gorgeous George, but unlike George, he didn't adopt the effeminate character traits. He was abrasive, mean, and nasty, and that formula made him a hit as a wrestler and a manager. Blassie also recorded the song "Pencil Neck Geek," long time favorite of novelty record collectors and fans of the Dr. Demento Show.

Blassie and his wife, a beautiful Asian woman he met while traveling the world, came over to the house many times to visit. He also sent my father letters, photos and postcards. I have a box of letters and photos, including some with Blassie's pet pythons, in my house today.

Mike Mazurki is another wrestler who became a life-long friend. Mazurki was born in Austria, and his family emigrated to the United States when he was six. He grew up in New York and became a professional football and basketball player as well as a wrestler. He was cast in a bit role in the film *The Shanghai Gesture* in 1941, and that opened the door to a long career in film and television. His film roles included *Dick Tracy*, *Murder, My Sweet*, and *Some Like It Hot*, and he guest starred on dozens of shows including *Gunsmoke*, *F-Troop*, *Gilligan's Island*, *The*

Beverly Hillbillies, *The Untouchables*, *Bonanza*, *The Munsters*, and *I Dream of Jeannie*.

Mazurki continued wrestling, even as his acting career took off. He co-founded the Cauliflower Alley Club in 1965 and became the first president of the wrestling association. Mike continued making films right up until his death, and one of his final roles was a cameo in Warren Beatty's *Dick Tracy*.

Vic and Ted Christy were good friends of my father as well. The two became a successful tag team in the 1950s, and Vic appeared as the villain in the movie *Challenge to be Free* alongside Mike Mazurki. Mazurki's character had a pet mountain lion in the film. Any time my Dad left the house, he would pay tribute to the film and to Mike by repeating the line spoken to the mountain lion, "Take care of the house, cat!"

Vic was a notorious practical joker, and Joe Jares captured a number of Vic's favorite games in his book *Whatever Happened to Gorgeous George?* One of Vic's favorite locker room stunts was to challenge guys to a feat of strength. Vic would have another wrestler stand with his heels and back to the wall, and Vic would try to pull the guy's head forward. Vic would pull and pull and pull while the other man strained to keep his head back, then at just the right moment, Vic would let go.

Vic was bold enough to pull a rib on the great Ed "Strangler" Lewis. He stuffed paper into the Strangler's boots one night and laughed to himself when Strangler started complaining that his boots felt too small.

Road trips in the wrestling business can be tedious affairs, and it was on the road that Vic pulled some of his tour audacious ribs. Once while driving with his brother Ted, the two pulled over on the side of the road. They opened the doors of the car, Ted laid across the hood, and Vic laid on the ground. When other drivers pulled over to help, the Christys would sit up and yell, "Can't we take a sunbath without being bothered by everybody?"

Another favorite of Vic's was pretending to strangle the driver of the car he was in when they passed other motorists. Vic thought it was funny, but his riding buddies weren't as amused when people would pull off the road and report a man being strangled in a car to the police.

Vic perfected the art of the "invisible driver" as well. he would sit in the front passenger seat, steer the car with his left hand on the lower part of the steering wheel, and stretch his left leg over to work the pedals. Joe Jares recalls seeing Christy pull alongside him and his father Frank during a road trip. Christy casually looked over and waved from the passenger seat as his invisible driver sped him away.

Vic was out by the pool at a Las Vegas hotel one time pushing people into the water. After making a nuisance of himself in his swimsuit, he went upstairs and came back in a suit. He grabbed fellow wrestler Nick Lutze and pushed him into the pool. Lutze had had enough of Vic's antics, so as soon as he got out of the water, he pushed Vic into the pool. Vic popped out of the water laughing. "You idiot, I'm wearing your suit!"

Dad also became acquainted with the legendary man of a thousand voices, Mel Blanc. Blanc was a regular on the Jack Benny program for years, and he was best known as the voice of almost all the

Looney Tune characters. My father loved Mel, and he painted an elaborate portrait for his friend. Mel was in the center of the painting, and all of his characters were in the painting surrounding his face. The painting hung in Mel's office until he died, and his son Noel has it now.

Dad was close friends with Mel's brother-in-law Rosie Rosenbaum. The two of them liked to travel together and made a number of trips to Russia. This would have been the late 1970s and early 1980s, when tensions were the highest between the then Soviet Union and the United States. My father brought me back several souvenirs from their 1980 trip to the Summer Olympics in Moscow, the year the US boycotted the games.

My father spoke lovingly of the Russian people and their way of life. I didn't realize it at the time, but he was quite the Soviet sympathizer. He liked the socialist ideals of the Soviets, and he often told me that he would gladly give up all his wealth if it meant that people would not go hungry or naked or homeless.

One of my father's dearest friends was Herb Jeffries. Herb was an actor, singer, and songwriter, and he was known as the first black cowboy singer, garnering nicknames like "The Bronze Buckaroo" and "The Sepia Singing Cowboy." Herb and my dad spent a lot of time hanging out at Muscle Beach, and my father the health nut had a lasting impact on Jeffries.

When I ran into Herb in 2010, he told me he owed his longevity to my father. Dad gave Herb the same lectures he always gave me about the evils of alcohol, drugs, and red meat, and Herb took them to heart. Herb was 97 years old when he told me all this, and when he passed away in 2014, he was nearing his 101st birthday.

One of the most unforgettable of my Dad's wrestling pals was a Greek grappler named Ted Tourtas. Ted developed a crush on my Aunt Paula, who we often referred to as the Zsa Zsa of the family. She was beautiful, glamorous, and flamboyant, and Ted took a liking to her. His obsession got the better of him one night when he tried to sneak in a window to get close to her. This was one of those windows that set above a doorway, and when Ted was half way through, he got stuck.

My father was a loyal and good friend to those who were good to him. But Paula was his sister, and needless to say, he was a little upset at Ted over that one!

Dad painted a number of celebrities, like actor Richard Boone.

Peter Falk as *Columbo*.

Charlie Chaplin.

NFL legend Lyle Alzado.

Above: The New York Jets and Atlanta Falcons.
Below: Ohio State vs. Michigan.

Above: A piece titled, *Down for the Count.*
Below: Hulk Hogan, painted in 1981.

BACK IN THE MAIN EVENT

For the remainder of 1952, Lord Carlton worked the Midwest, the Northeast, and the Southeast against the biggest names in the business. In November Carlton dropped a match to Jim Londos, the Greek Adonis who ruled the wrestling world during the 1930s. That same month, he had one of his earliest encounters with Zebra Kid, and unusual masked grappler whose mask and cape bore the signature stripes of the African beast. George Bollas was the original and most famous Zebra Kid, but when Lord Carlton met him in 1952, it was Lenny Montana under the mask. Lord Carlton also faced "Mr. America" Gene Stanlee in Washington, D.C., and he dropped a match to old rival Antonino Rocca in Teaneck, New Jersey.

In December Lord Carlton found himself in the title picture in Georgia, battling Don McIntyre for his NWA Southern Heavyweight Championship. Carlton was unable to take the belt from the champion, but it didn't matter. His status as a top heel and main event talent made him a draw, win or lose.

Promoters and wrestlers had a good business model going in the 1950s. The National Wrestling Alliance had a stranglehold on the business. Alliance members, who represented just about every territory in the United States and Canada, were able to restrict competition and threats to their business. Members respected the territorial boundaries of one another. They rotated and traded talent to keep fresh faces coming in to their towns. They shared a world champion and made sure big names like Lord Carlton moved from place to place so that their fellow promoters could benefit from the drawing power. If someone dared try to run against an Alliance member in their cities, Alliance members would send in their best stars to crush the competition.

Not everyone was happy with this arrangement, especially wrestlers who worked with the "outlaw" promotions and found themselves blackballed from NWA promotions. Occasionally a jilted wrestler or a crooked promoter looking to make a buck would slip a story to the media, threatening to blow the whistle on the NWA and its twisted ways.

In 1953, Lord Carlton earned a mention in one such whistle blower story printed by the *Police Gazette*. The *Gazette* was an early supporter and promoter of wrestling dating back to the late 1800s, but in 1953, they ran an interview with police Sgt. Henry Wittenberg, who made some huge claims about promises made to him by those in the professional wrestling business.

Wittenberg was an Olympic champion who boasted a record of over 500 victories without a loss. His wrestling prowess attracted the attention of New York wrestling impresario Toots Mondt, who wanted to make him a star.

In the article, titled "Why I Refuse to Become a Mat Freak," Wittenberg claims Mondt offered him $15,000 and a cut at the gate. Lord Carlton, he claimed, said the two of them could easily clear $50,000 if they toured together.

Wittenberg went on, saying that Mondt wanted him to win the title from Antonino Rocca at Madison Square Garden in his first match. Rocca would then retire to his native Argentina but later demand a rematch. That match would take place in Argentina, and Mondt, Wittenberg claims, estimated the gate could clear over a million dollars.

Wittenberg painted himself as the victim, a man of great character who refused to stoop to something so low as my father's brand of wrestling. "When I wrestle, I wrestle to win. I won't become a mat freak! If I turned pro, I could wrestle Primo Carnera and Tony Galento at the same time. But my conscience wouldn't let me."

Noble as Wittenburg's posturing may be, the facts are the facts. The "real" champion of wrestling, as the *Gazette* proclaimed Wittnberg to be, spent his days patrolling the streets while Mondt, my father, Carnera, Galento, and Rocca made real money as mat freaks.

Lord Carlton wrapped up his eastern tour and headed back west in the summer of 1953, working the Southwest and California. Fans in both places had not forgotten his lordship or the Swami, and they showed up in droves to see the British champion. Lord Carlton also made his triumphant return to the hottest program on TV, *Wrestling from Hollywood*, when he returned to the Olympic.

On August 19 in Tucson, Lord Carlton stepped into the ring for what had to be one of the most colorful and over the top affairs in wrestling to date. Lord Carlton, with his Swami at his side and his colorful robes, would go face to face with the other spirit child of Lord Lansdowne, Gorgeous George. Angelo Martinelli was booked to face a mystery man known as the Masked Stranger in the opener and Mildred Burke, the Women's World Champion, was booked just beneath the boys in a two out of three falls title match against Cora Combs, making this truly a one of a kind super card.

The promoter made sure to note that having such high profile wrestlers meant that the guaranteed pay outs for the show would be higher. Thus it became necessary for one night to raise prices. Fans eagerly lined up to see not only the two most flamboyant male wrestlers of the day, but also two of the toughest, hardest hitting women in the game.

A crowd of 3,600 showed up for the biggest show of the year, but they were disappointed that only Burke was able to win a decisive victory. Martinelli won one fall against the Masked Stranger, but he was unable to get a second or unmask his foe before time expired.

As for the main event, Gorgeous George made his entrance wearing a new robe he called "Sunset Over Old Arizona." Lord Carlton protested Jeffrey's presence at ringside, saying that Jeffrey did not have a license but the Swami did. Referee Monte LaDue ignored Carlton's protests, and the match went on. Both men were able to score a pin fall, but when their brawl spilled out of the ring, they were both counted out in a double disqualification.

Lord Carlton finished out the year doing battle with more of the top stars of the day. He scored victories over Wee Willie Davis, Leo Garibaldi, and Warren Bockwinkel while losing a December battle against Sando Szabo.

By November he was back in Los Angeles, and had a regular spot on the television program *Wrestling From Hollywood*. In January he renewed his rivalry with legitimate British star Lord Blears in a series of matches, including a February tag match with the Swami as Lord Carlton's partner. Dad and the Swami faced off against Lord Blears and his partner Wilbur Snyder, a former football player who went on to become a tag champion with Dick the Bruiser in the American Wrestling Association before becoming one of the top guys alongside Bruiser in the World Wrestling Association in Indianapolis, Indiana. Snyder and Blears defeated Lord Carlton and the Swami in two out of three falls.

Carlton wrestled Bobo Brazil in March of 1954. The match went the distance with no victor, allowing my father to once again give the rub to a rising African-American star who would become a national star.

WRESTLING Thurs. Night
Municipal Auditorium

MAIN EVENT
TAG-TEAM MATCH
Lord Carlton & Hindu Swami
vs.
Lord Blears & Wilbur Snyder

Semi-Main
Bud CURTIS vs. Gori GUERREO
Plus
2 Other Star Bouts

Lord Carlton and the Swami tagged a few times in the mid 1950s. Note Gory Guerrero, patriarch of the Guerrero wrestling family, is also on the card.

Dad wore the monocle well, don't you think?

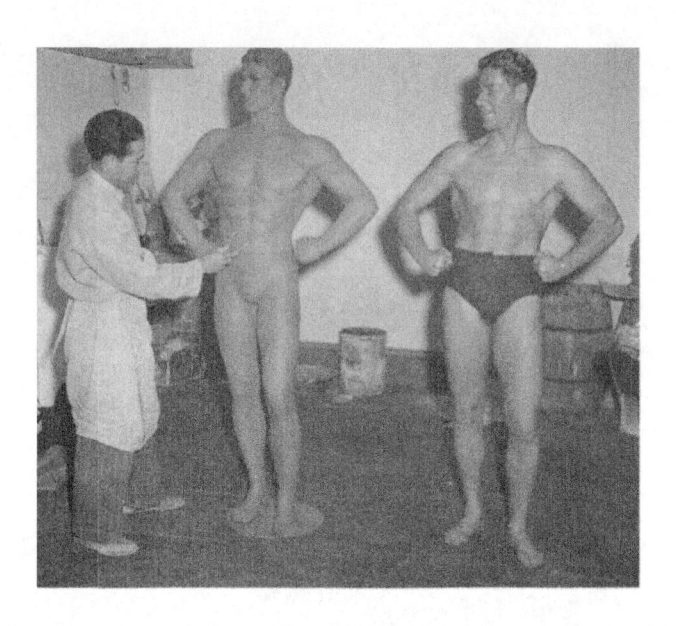

There's a part of me that wants to know where this mannequin is. A larger part of me is a little creeped out by it.

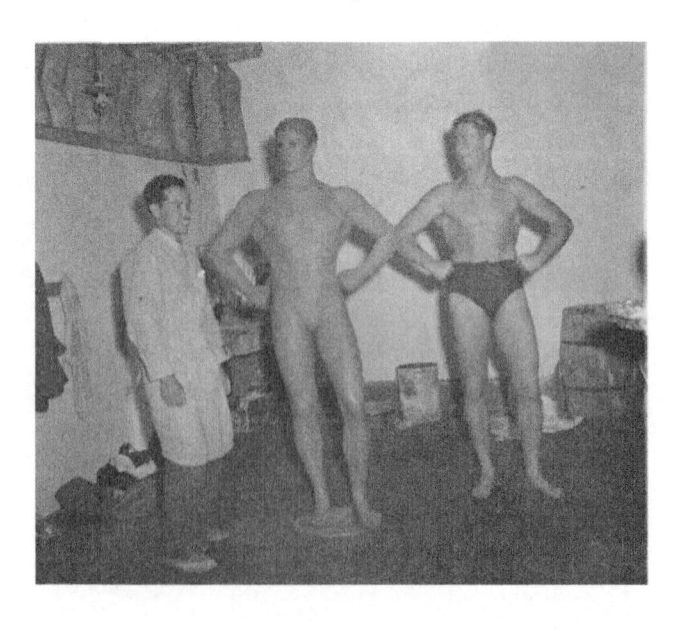

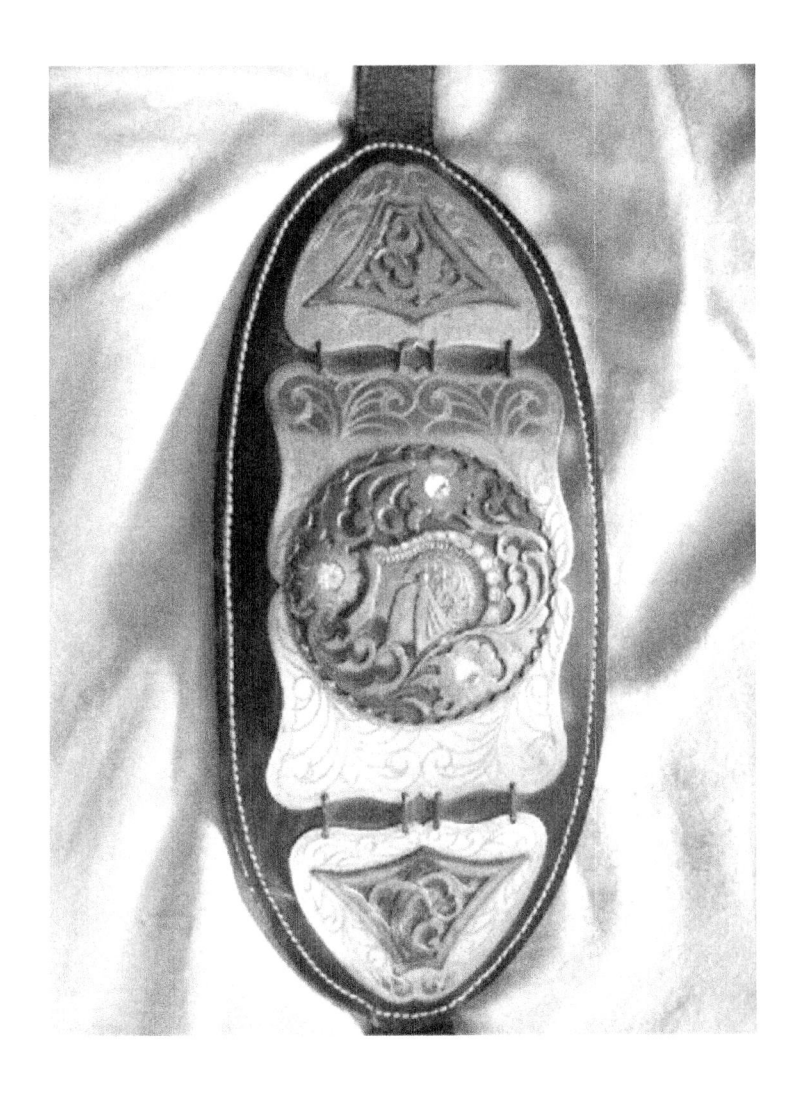

A mystery title belt from my father's personal collection.

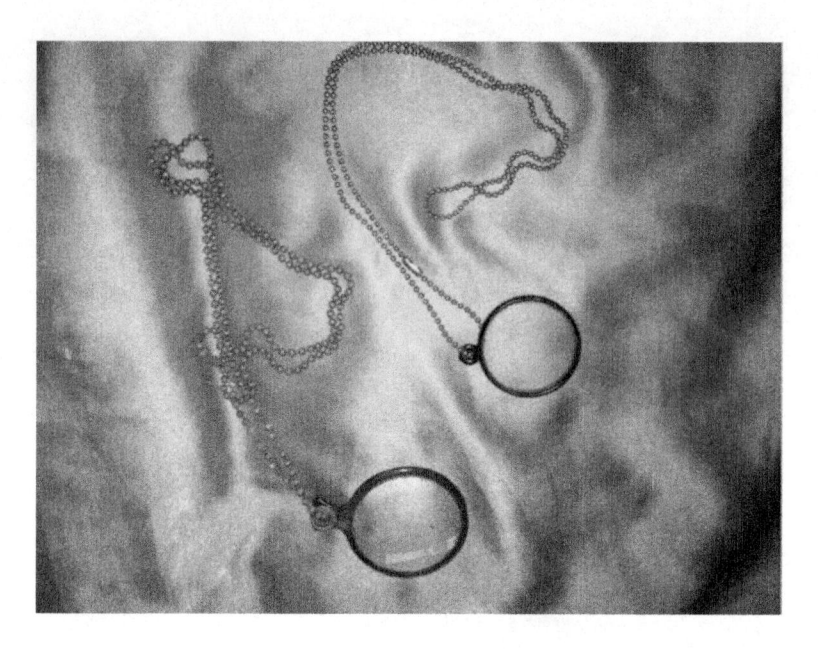

Above: A pair of monocles used during his Lordship's years in the ring. Below: Lord Carlton with his car and entourage. Courtesy Jim Oetkins.

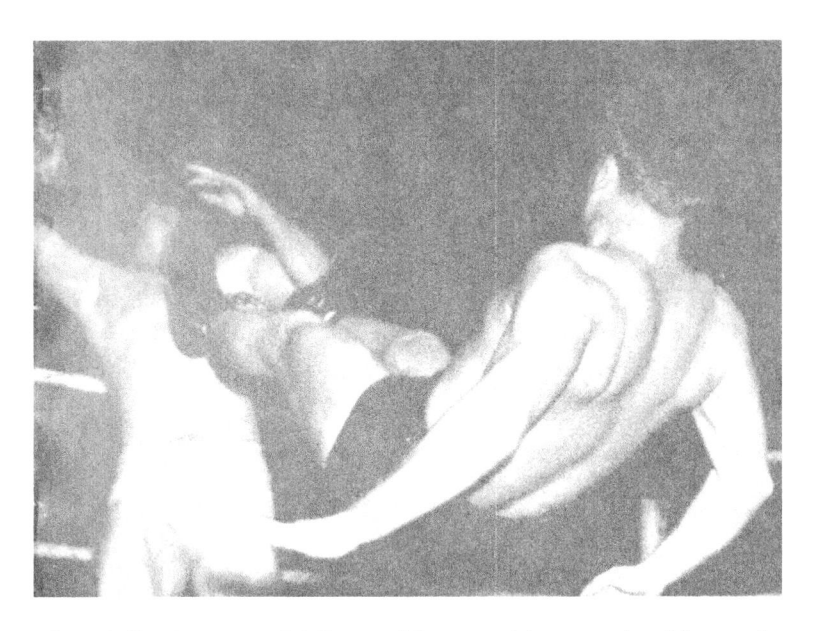

Lord Carlton could fly and he could grapple. Most of his opponents never had a chance!

Lord Leslie Carlton sans robe and monocle in 1952.

LEAVING HIS MARK

In the summer of 1954, Lord Carlton took a long overdue break from the wrestling scene. He had been working for nearly fifteen years, traveling the country, appearing on television, and working with the biggest names in the business. He took about six months off before returning in December.

As Lord Carlton, my father never got a run with a major world title. Lou Thesz was the NWA champion for most of the 1950s, and Thesz was very protective of the belt and the image it represented. Even though wrestling had long ceased to be a legitimate sport, it was important to Thesz and many others in the NWA that the champion be someone the public viewed as a thoroughly legitimate grappler.

Thesz traveled from territory to territory defending his belt against the top guy. He was a guaranteed draw based on his title and his stature in the business. But men like my father, Gorgeous George, and Buddy Rogers (whom Thesz especially disliked) did not need title belts. Their charisma and reputations made them solid money makers.

Lord Carlton would work a few territories in his remaining years in the business, but he was also in demand as a special attraction. It was not uncommon for him to be in New Mexico one week and Oregon the next.

Late 1954 saw Lord Carlton travel back to the Southwest and the East Coast. He continued working with Primo Carnera, Antonino Rocca, and Jack Claybourne and took on new faces like Tony Galento.

The year 1955 saw Lord Carlton traveling from one coast to the other, appearing in rings across the country. He did television in California, New York, and Las Vegas. He also worked the Southwestern territory of Arizona and New Mexico, the Pacific Northwest, and Illinois. He fell into a short term program with California wrestler Matt Murphy in April, but for the most part he and the Swami were simply globe trotters, going where they were booked and drawing money in the main event.

Like the champion Thesz, Lord Carlton's opponents were typically the top talent in each regional promotion or other national stars. Carlton often appeared along side Gene "Mr. America" Stanlee, Gorgeous George, Hans Schnabel, Antonino Rocca, and Primo Carnera.

In the fall of 1955 Lord Carlton had two more confrontations with Gorgeous George. *The Los Angeles Times* TV listings for September 15 promised TV viewers a mud match between the two in Las Vegas. On October 25 Carlton and George met at the South Gate Arena in Los Angeles for two out of three falls main event. George and Carlton were tied at one fall each when the action spilled out of the ring and into the crowd. Both men were counted out, and the match was called a draw.

Carlton ran up against a unique opponent in November in the form of Elephant Boy. Elephant Boy was a creation of Jack Pfefer, who also billed him as the Wildman of Borneo in an attempt to cash in on fans who wouldn't know the difference between his man and the more famous Wildman of Borneo. Elephant Boy was a wild looking character with big hair and a big bear who wore tiger-striped trunks. He also had an equalizer to Lord Carlton's Swami, the Slave Girl. Slave Girl wore an animal print dress, and though tiny, she could fight with anyone, male or female.

Elephant Boy, real name William Olivas, eventually left the business and became a Roman Catholic priest. Slave Girl stayed in the business until the day she died. Her real name was Lillian Ellison, but fans came to know her best as The Fabulous Moolah.

The match against Elephant Boy ended the way most fans probably hoped: as a complete melee. Carlton and Elephant Boy traded falls, but before a third and deciding fall could happen, both the Swami and Slave Girl hit the ring for a free for all.

Lord Carlton's rarely lost a match in those days. If he didn't win honestly (and he rarely did), he usually won by some dirty deeds on the part of the Swami. Carlton took the third and deciding fall against African American star Jack Clayborne on November 2, 1995, when the Swami reached into the ring and tripped Clayborne, allowing Carlton to get the deciding pin fall.

Most of the marquee matchups with other top stars ended in a double disqualification tied at one fall a piece or a time limit draw. As unsatisfying as such a result could be to a crowd, it was often the best to way for a heel like Lord Carlton to keep his heat while not diminishing the momentum of his babyface opponent. The crowd left angry but primed to pay big money for the next time someone promised to put the dastardly Lord Carlton in his place.

1955 was also the year the Federal government stepped up their investigation into the National Wrestling Alliance, the governing body of professional wrestling. The Alliance divided the country up into thirty different territories with members controlling each region. The members of the Alliance colluded with one another to restrict competition within their borders, and they made sure that anyone who ran in such territories not only did so with their blessing but paid the NWA a handsome portion of their winnings.

The NWA also worked hard to insure that the wrestlers who worked for the NWA did not work for what they considered to be outlaw promotions. Promoters locked talent into contracts that gave the promoters a major cut of their earnings and kept them from working for the outlaws. Wrestlers who did not tow the line were blackballed and found it hard to get work.

As early as 1953, my father's name was on a list of wrestlers believed to have been blackballed in certain territories for disobeying the will of the NWA. A wrestling promoter and fellow Hungarian named Nick Lutze went to the FBI on April 14 of that year with a story of how LA promoters Cal Eaton and Johnny Doyle manipulated television contracts and wrestlers to force Lutze out of business. Lutze named several wrestlers, including my father and Primo Carnera, as men whose careers were threatened if they wrestled for Lutze.

It wasn't until 1955 that investigator Stanley Disney sat down with my father to get his side of the story. Disney also found willing witnesses in the likes of former women's champ Mildred Burke and promoter Jack Pfefer who were more than glad to spill the beans on the NWA's darkest secrets.

Pfefer was a meticulous record keeper who never threw anything away. His files were jammed with letters and documents about every wrestler and promoter he ever worked with, and he often used his extensive documentation to bully people into giving him his way. Pfefer drew a black cat on the file folders of people who rubbed him the wrong way, and he was not above exposing the business if a promoter would not pay Pfefer what he believed was his due. Pfefer's love of dirt and penchant for blackmail had a positive pay off in the end. His records, now housed at the University of Notre Dame library, left us with a treasure chest of information about wrestling's golden age.

Whatever stories my father told the government, they weren't enough to damage his career. Lord Carlton was a guaranteed draw at the box office, and as long as he was willing to lace up the boots, he had no trouble finding someone willing to put him on the card.

Wilbur Snyder, Sandor Szabo, and Primo Carnera continued to be Carlton's most frequent opponents going into 1956. Carnera and Carlton renewed their old rivalry in the place it began, down in the Southwest before taking the feud to California. Carnera was one of the few men who could score a pin fall against his lordship. Carlton would get one back for every win Carnera took, a sign of respect between two old veterans who had countless matches together.

Lord Carlton also reunited with an old rival from England, the legitimate Brit Lord Blears. The two noblemen paired up and became a tag team in 1957 and won the NWA International Tag Team Titles. They dropped the titles in March to Gene Stanlee and Sandor Szabo.

Lord Carlton renewed his rivalry with Gorgeous George on June 8, 1957 in San Benardino. This time there would be no draw. Gorgeous George took the first fall in 15 minutes 55 seconds with a hip roll, and Lord Carlton would answer 49 seconds later with a drop kick that resulted in a pin fall. The Human Orchid appeared to have the deciding fall locked up when he put Lord Carlton into a submission hold, but Carlton tricked George into loosening his grip and took advantage, pinning the Gorgeous One for the win.

It's worth noting that both my father and Gorgeous George were singled out by New York writer Robert Ruark in a 1950 piece that ran in newspapers across the country sarcastically calling for bull fighting to be broadcast on television. Ruark took exception to the "sadism" he saw in television's early fascination with roller derby, ice hockey, and professional wrestling, and suggested that if such abominations were allowed to be broadcast, the ban on bullfighting might as well be lifted too.

"The freaks and monsters who live by professional wrestling were distasteful enough to anyone with a finicky stomach in the old says. I supposed that a burger who wears a monocle, bills himself as "Lord Carlton," and describes himself as a British noble is easily the cultural superior or any one of the numerous angels. But I am inclined to cavil a touch at Gorgeous George, with his scent, his marcelled hair, and the mock daintiness which lends and extra neurotic bang to his performance.

"You cannot dignify wrestling, skating derbies, or professional hockey as sport... They are outlets for those who find peculiar satisfaction in simulated or real pain at the expense of other people. This is sadism."

I don't know if my father ever read Ruark's column, but I am sure he would have been proud at the mention!

WRESTLING
OLYMPIA STADIUM
FRI., DEC. 9, 1955
8:30 P. M.

After more than two and a half years, the feud between Antonino Rocca and Lord Carlton still boils and seethes. That's why their return match at the Olympia tonight promises to be one of the outstanding wrestling matches of any year.

Rocca met Lord Carlton here in March, 1953, in a set-to that is still vividly remembered as one of the most savage encounters in the annals of the mat game in Detroit. These two muscular giants battled for a solid hour, with neither gaining any perceptible advantage.

After 60 minutes of unremitting ring warfare, the match was declared a draw. This outcome satisfied nobody. It enraged the fans, most of whom were solidly behind the athletic and sportsmanlike Rocca. Even more enraged was Lord Carlton, who blamed the meddling of the referee for his frustration.

Ever since that night, Olympia officials have been trying to get Rocca and Lord Carlton back in the same ring. The official explanation of the long delay is that recurring conflicts in schedules made it impossible for the two wrestling greats and the Olympia to arrive at a mutually acceptable date any earlier.

Rocca and Lord Carlton, however, have carried their antagonism for each other outside the ring with charges and counter charges. Each insists that the other has been dodging his challenges for the last 32 months.

"I've been willing to wrestle Lord Carlton any time, any where, under any terms," says Rocca. "I would have whipped him the first time if the referee hadn't let him break every rule in the book. I'll take him on this time, anything goes, and show who's boss."

Lord Carlton has similar ideas.

"Rocca has been running away from me for nearly three years," says His Lordship. "I don't blame him. I'd run, too, if I was Rocca. Now that he has made the mistake of signing to meet me again, I'll show what an overrated wrestler he is. I'll pin him inside of 20 minutes."

The second meeting will be a match to one fall, with an hour's time limit. Both Rocca and Lord Carlton agree on one thing—this is one scrap that won't last the full distance. And that's about the only thing on which the two rivals do agree.

Nice write up in a wrestling program for a re-match between Lord Carlton and Antonino Rocca.

LORD CARLTON

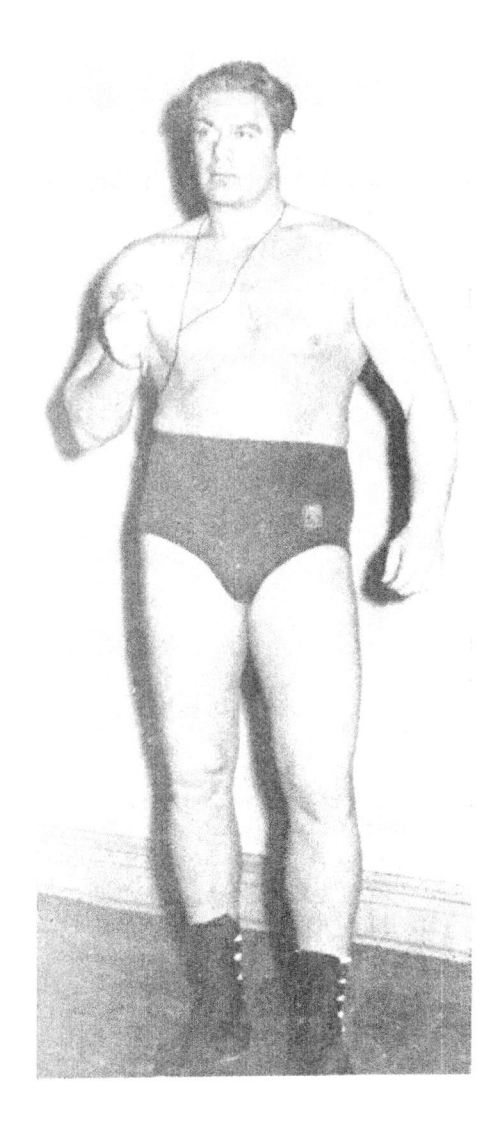

A photo of Lord Carlton from the Olympia program.

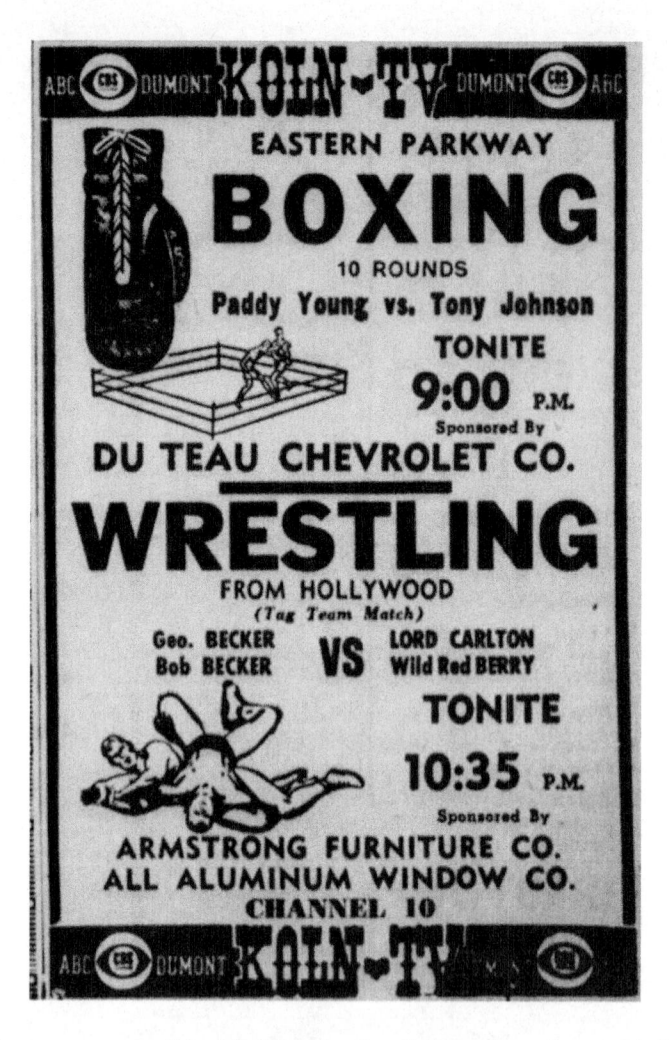

Newspaper ad in Nebraska for *Wrestling from Hollywood*.

Nice photo ad from New Mexico, fall of 1955.

June 1957, when my father defeated Gorgeous George.

GOING OUT IN STYLE

Wrestling fans today would be shocked to see the golden age of wrestling in Los Angeles. By the late 1950s, wrestling was so popular, there were 1-3 shows every night within an 80 mile radius of Los Angeles. Every town had an arena built almost exclusively for wrestling with permanent rings, an entry way, and sloped seating areas that could hold around 1800. The Olympic in Los Angeles had a trap door beneath the ring so that wrestlers could escape a fan melee in a pinch. The fact that such incidents happened often enough to necessitate such an escape route speaks to how much the people believed in what they saw!

Even with wrestling on television every night, fans still packed the arenas. Promoters were making a killing. After paying building rentals and other expenses, good house could net you $2000 easily. Wrestlers were getting paid well too. At a time when the starting salary was around $1.00 per hour, they were guaranteed a minimum of $25 a night. Top stars made far more than that, and some became extremely wealthy. When Baron Leone passed, he left millions in his estate.

Despite their above average minimum pay, Not everyone was satisfied. A few of the boys ran the numbers and quickly realized that promoters were not sharing the wealth. A savvy promoter could put on a show with only six wrestlers. Two singles matches would open the show beginning at 8:30. The winners and losers would pair up for a tag match. A two-out-of-three falls match would be the main event, and the show would wrap by 10 pm.

Once the doors were locked, the promoter doled out the night's payouts: $25 per undercard worker, $25 for an official, and $35 each for the main event workers. Everyone's making more than the average Californian, but the promoter is taking home $1800 for himself!

Lord Carlton was one of about twenty men who took exception to the inequality exercised by LA's most powerful wrestling promotion, NWA member Hollywood Wrestling. When the office refused to increase their pay, they left to start their own promotion. The men involved in the revolt were immediately blackballed by the NWA, but in wrestling-crazy Southern California, they had no trouble finding a crowd.

"Lord Carlton was the big name," says Karl Lauer. "He was a huge star everywhere he went. When they left Hollywood Wrestling, he had a very memorable run with Matt Murphy. They must have gone on for several weeks with that feud. This was in the days before wrestlers got 'color,' all the time. You rarely saw blood, and it was only done if the house was big and a feud was wrapping up. Lord Carlton was one of the first to use color, and he knew how to get just enough to bring the fans to the edge of their seats."

Lauer says the outlaw promotion was so successful, they nearly got their own television program. Sadly, the promotion didn't last long enough to get the deal done. "They couldn't get booked anywhere else. The NWA was too powerful. One by one, they all went back and made amends. The only one who didn't was Lord Carlton."

By 1958 Lord Carlton knew his time in the wrestling business was coming to a close, but he was not prepared to go quietly. Working in the Southwestern United States territories including California, New Mexico, and Arizona, Lord Carlton continued to receive top billing while putting over young stars. An April 22 battle with Danny O'Shocker in Tucson was ruled a draw when a riot broke out involving three wrestlers, two referees, and a number of fans. The match was tied at one fall a piece, and after several minutes of brawling, referee Paavo Ketonen called a draw.

As violent as that night was, it paled in comparison to Lord Carlton's October match up with Phil Melby. Melby was a fixture in the Arizona territory for decades. He wrestled both Gorgeous George (whom he defeated) and Lou Thesz (whom he did not defeat). While my father was winding down his career, Melby was just getting started. He would remain a popular wrestler Mexico and the Southwest until his retirement in 1986.

On October 21 the two met at Tucson Garden in a Texas Death Match. "There will be no disqualifications and pin falls do not count," the *Tucson Daily Citizen* proclaimed on the day of the bout. "A wrestler cannot be counted out of the ring, and the match will not be stopped for injuries. The winner must leave the ring under his own power, and a contender must answer the bell after a 30-second rest period following a fall, or give up."

Melby got the win that night, but he and many others paid the price. The fight spilled out into the crowd, and the fans got involved. A riot broke out in the Arena involving the fans and other wrestlers along with Melby and Carlton, who were both a bloody mess by the end of the bout. Arizona wrestling historian Dale Pierce says it still stands as one of the most memorable nights in the state's wrestling history. What a way to cap a career.

By 1959 Lord Carlton was off the road, but he was not quickly forgotten. A wrestler in the Carolinas decided to carry on the name for himself in 1959. He was billed as Little Lord Carlton, and yes, he was a midget!

No wrestler ever truly goes away for good, of course, and Lord Leslie Carlton was no exception. Four year later, he came back to do a brief feud with Gene "Mr. America" Stanlee. Wrestlingdata.com lists a February 28, 1962 tag match in which Carlton and Jerry Graham lost to Gene Stanlee and Kiko Torres as his last match, but Stanlee and Carlton stretched their feud out over a handful of singles and tag matches after that event.

The Salt Lake Tribune may hold the key to Lord Carlton's final match. It took place on April 20, 1962, and pitted his lordship, the British champion, against his long time rival Primo Carnera.

Lord Carlton vs. Bobo Brazil, January 1957.

LORD LESLIE CARLTON
Meets O'Shocker Tonight

Before his 1958 riot-inducing battle with Danny O'Shocker, still in tip top shape!

PHIL MELBY
Meets Lord Carlton

Lord Carlton's foe for a bloody Texas Death Match brawl in 1958.

WRESTLING
Special
PRIMO CARNERA
Ex-World's Heavyweight Boxing Champ
VS.
LORD CARLTON
British Empire Champion
GRAHAM vs. **FLETCHER**
PAUL DeGALLIS
Good Supporting Card
COLISEUM
Friday — 8:30
50¢—$1.00—$1.25—$1.50

One final match against his old nemesis, Primo Carnera. Utah, 1962.

A NEW BEGINNING

You often hear stories of athletes who end up penniless after their retirement. Football, basketball, baseball stars, even wrestlers spend more than they make while they're on top of the world. They live for the moment, giving no thought at all to the future, and when the future finally comes, they find they have nothing left.

Not so with my father, or many wrestlers of his generation. These were children of the depression, and they knew the value of a penny. There are exceptions to every rule, but these men by and large were thrifty, stretching every dollar as far as it could go. They carpooled, they lived off bologna and bread, they slept in their cars, and at the end of the day, they retired like kings.

Baron Michele Leone was able to live the life of a baron after he retired. He owned an apartment complex aptly named, The Baron's Castle. He and his wife spent three decades living in the Castle, enjoying walks on the beach and traveling whenever they pleased.

Just down the street from the Castle was an apartment complex that to this day bears the name "Lord Carlton." It was the first of many such investments my father would make over the years. He was always looking for a new deal, a new opportunity, a new place to invest in the future.

Lou D'Elia was only eight years old when his family moved into Lord Carlton's building. He, like all his tenants, knew my father by his original ring name, Tug. "The first thing he did was put a water fountain out front. He was crazy about water features, and every building he bought, he installed one. The one in front of my building had a statue of David and a big pond in front. He also put a mini-alligator in the pond. I told him he was crazy to put that thing in the pond because it would get stolen. It wasn't a great neighborhood, and I was always getting my toys stolen. But he was clever enough to attach a chain to the alligator, attaching it to the bottom of the pond. It was very eccentric, and I really liked him."

My father returned to his first passion, art, as soon as he was settled in the new place. "He lived in the back of the building," says D'Elia, "And he had another unit he kept for himself just for his painting. He loved to share his art with me."

My father was on his second marriage when retirement began. My mother was a Hungarian immigrant named Gwendolyn, and my father met her when she was dancing with the Radio City Rockettes. He was 37 when they were married; she was only 17. Dad called her Pixie.

"She had bright red hair, and she was very loud," remembers Lou D'Elia. "Kind of like Bette Midler. You could tell right away she ruled the roost. Tug almost always let her have her way. He was a big man, but he was also a very gentle man."

One of my father's good friends in his post-wrestling years was Johnny Andriolo. Johnny met my father and mother in 1966, and he remained friends with them until my father's death in 1988. "No one called me Johnny except Tug and Pixie. Everyone else knows me as John. And when I met my wife Rosemarie, they started calling her Rosemary."

Johnny and Rosemary were frequent guests in our house, and they loved both of my parents. "From the moment I met them, I knew they were friends for life. And I was so glad my wife fell in with them too. We would drop in on them every two or three weeks, and we had some of the best times telling stories and laughing. Rosemary and I would bring food over to the house, or we'd invite them to join us at a fun spot we had found."

Tug and Pixie's first son was my brother Kitt, whom I always called Pig. He grew up to be a nuclear scientist. Dad got custody of Ricky after Kitt was born, and then they had my other brother Cleet, whom I always called Shoe. I was the baby of the family.

"Kitt was a year younger than me," says Lou. "We played together a lot. He would take us to the beach, or to a club to go swimming. I didn't know Ricky well, but I recall he was a pretty good swimmer. Tug pushed all of his boys in sports, really hard. I wondered later if that might have been part of what went wrong with Ricky."

My father was a very regimented man, and he lived on a very strict schedule. He got up at 11 AM every day, and he went to sleep at 2 AM after the late night shows. He painted every evening, and his daily activities varied depending on what day of the week it was.

My father had very little tolerance for people who didn't take care of themselves. He wanted to be healthy, but at the same time he had a serious aversion to doctors. If he or someone he knew had a medical problem, Tug wanted to solve it himself.

Tug had a friend who had a cyst on his hand. Tug pulled a giant medical encyclopedia off the bookshelf and opened it up.

"Lay your hand flat on the table, with the cyst facing up," my father said. His friend did it, and my father brought that encyclopedia down hard on the man's hand, right on top of the cyst!

As his friend nursed his sore hand, my father told him that the impact would break up the cyst and it would dissipate through his body. Dad was right; the cyst was gone in days.

Dad didn't believe in pain killers much either. When he went to the dentist, he refused to be given any Novocain, telling the doctor that Novocain was for sissies.

Dad was also quite phobic about germs. He told me a story once about going on a date to the movies with a very pretty girl. The girl bought a candy bar, unwrapped it, and handed it to my father with her bare hands. He never took her out again.

"Your body is a temple," he used to say to me. "Your mouth is the gateway to that temple, and there are more germs on your fingers than there are on a monkey's ass."

Dad had many sayings like this he repeated over and over. When I was learning to drive he taught me this lesson. "If you're driving down a road, and you have to swerve to miss something in the road, and you see a pack of prize-winning dogs to the left, and a drunken, sick man to the right, always aim for the dogs."

No, my father didn't hate animals, but he valued human life above animals and truly cared for people. The same cannot be said of my older brother Kitt, who had his own version of the story. "If you see a pair of flea-bitten dogs on one side and a world champion wrestler on the other, knock his kangaroo boots into the trees!"

I don't think my brother was an animal lover near as much as he was a hater of my father.

One time dad traded a Rolex watch to a man for a Shetland pony and a colt. The pony was mine, and the colt belonged to Kitt. Kitt loved that colt, and the animal was very sweet, but the pony was nothing but trouble. The pony figured out how to untie the ropes we used to tie them up, and the pony would wander off to the lake. The colt would follow, because that's just what horses do.

My father became extremely frustrated with the animals, and he called the man he had given the Rolex to see if he would take them back. "I'm very sorry," said the man, "I no longer have the Rolex."

"Did I ask for the Rolex back?" my father replied.

I was sad to see my pony go, but about six months later, I bought another pony with some money I had saved. I've never been without horses since. Kitt never had another pet, and I don't think he ever got over losing the colt.

Johnny Andriolo and his wife were animal lovers themselves and became dog breeders, competing in the Westminster Kennel Club competitions for years with champion Mastiffs. "We named our kennel Lord Carlton's Mastiffs, and our first two dogs were Tug and Pixie."

Sorry if this sounds harsh, but it gives me no end of joy knowing that there was a bitch out there named after my mom!

My mom liked game shows, and she once went on *Name that Tune* as a contestant. She did very well and was on her way to winning a brand new car, but she blew the final question. The song that stumped her was "The Sound of Silence," which was my father's favorite song. Sounds surprising, unless you know that deep down, my mother despised everything about my father.

According to one of my brothers, my father decided he wanted to move to a houseboat. He wanted to sell everything, get away from it all, and live on a houseboat. It was shortly after announcing these plans, my mother told him she was pregnant with me. This, my brother says, was her way of ruining my father's plans.

Mom could put on a good front for just about everyone, but growing under the same roof with the two of them, it was very apparent she despised my father. She was constantly looking for little ways to needle him and put a wedge between him and his children. She hated him and everything he loved.

"We never knew about any animosity between Tug and Pixie," says Johnny Andriolo. "We always had a wonderful time any chance we got to see them."

My father still got his houseboat. It wasn't a big one, but he loved it dearly. He referred to it as his "Tugboat." Dad bought it from a company called Camp or Cruise, and it was a one of a kind. They made a second boat identical to my dad's, but for some reason it was recalled to the factory and destroyed.

The man Tug bought the boat from was named, I kid you not, Bob Suninshine. (I may be spelling that wrong!) He and my father became dear friends, and Bob loved to brag he was pals with Lord Carlton. It drove my mother nuts to hear him tell stories about hanging around my dad and even scoring a win over him in an impromptu wrestling match.

Tug put a larger engine into the house boat because he wanted it to go faster. He wasn't pleased with the results, so he shifted the weights in the bottom of the boat to lift the front end out of the water and reduce drag. The boat had a diving board sticking out the front, and it listed to one side because the weights weren't evenly redistributed beneath. It looked like a sick dog with its tongue hanging out sitting in the water, but it was fast enough to pull a water skier. Of course when he did get it up to speed, all the doors would fly open, and anything not tied down would come flying out the back of the boat.

"Look!" my dad would brag. "Everyone's watching! They can't believe how fast this thing can go!"

"No," said Cleet. "That's *not* why they're staring!"

My father loved that boat. He had it repainted every year. He was cheap, and he used house paint, which never lasted, so it was really out of necessity that he paint it as often as he did. He kept the boat the rest of his life, and it was one of the first things my mother sold after he passed.

My mother got her big house wish too when Dad moved us to a nice house on a about fourteen acres of land. Given my mother's terrible treatment, it's a small wonder my father chose to live in his own private wing of the house. He had his own living space, his art studio, his favorite couch, and a giant TV. He had a king sized bed all his own, and a giant painting of San Francisco hung over that bed. That painting is in my bedroom today.

All his life, Tug never drank, never smoked, and he stayed away from red meat. He couldn't understand people who gave in to any of these vices, and lectured me and my mother to follow his example. Mom honored his request by smoking and drinking as much as she could when he was out of sight. She had alcohol stashed in all corners of the house. She used to pour vodka into milk to hide the scent. Innocent little me happened upon one of those glasses of milk one time and got a nasty surprise when I decided to take a sip!

"One time we came over for dinner," says Johnny Andriolo. "We were having spaghetti, and Rosemary and I brought a big bottle of red wine. We were enjoying ourselves, laughing and cutting up. All of a sudden, Tug stands up. He's limping badly, because he hadn't had his first hip surgery yet, and he grabs the bottle of wine. He walks down the hall to the bathroom. A few seconds later, we hear a flush. He comes back out with an empty bottle. Were were all getting a little too loud, so Tug went and poured out the rest of the wine. That only made us laugh harder."

My father stumbled on my mother's booze several times. Any time he found alcohol, he poured it out, but Mom soon discovered a way to keep her stash safe. Dad was 6'4". He had a bad limp and a bad hip that prevented him from bending down very far. In fact, when he sat to the dinner table, we scooted the table to him, since when he would scoot a chair towards the table it wasn't uncommon for him to break the arms off his chair in the attempt. Once Mom realized that he could look high but not low, all she had to do was hide her drink in the lower cabinets. She knew he'd never find it.

I often wondered why he didn't simply divorce my mother. I finally asked him once and he told me, "Her lies are better than my truth." Dad knew if they ended up in divorce court, she would demolish him with her gift for fiction. He had no desire to go through a divorce or the trial that would ensue.

I think his first wife Peggy was an even bigger reason why he stayed. He never told me what went wrong in their marriage, but I could tell he felt some guilt over it. Whatever happened with Peggy, it was reason enough for him to be stubborn and stick with my mother no matter what.

On one of my father's trips to Russia, my dad sent a postcard to my Aunt Paula that said he had left my mother and relocated to Russia. He wanted Paula to leave the postcard out so that Ricky, who frequently dropped in on Paula, would see it. My father was afraid of Ricky after what happened with Peggy, and I think it was his way of protecting us.

"Ricky was a great swimmer when he was younger," says Johnny Andriolo. "Tug was a good swimmer, and he's the one who taught Ricky. Ricky won a lot of championships when he was in his early teens, but he just wasn't into it. He made a joke of things, and he was more interested in getting high than winning championships.

"I know Tug loved him, and he wanted to hand over all his real estate to Ricky. His business was worth millions even then. After what happened to his wife, he just couldn't do it."

My father was truly devastated by murder. He was heartbroken for his ex-wife and also for his son. Ricky was a deeply religious man, but he very likely had some sort of mental issues going on as well. His ex-wife Pauline says that whatever money he made he would give away. He had a generous heart, but that generosity meant he was giving away the money Pauline needed to care for their daughter Lisa.

I still keep in touch with Pauline and Lisa. Pauline told me that when she re-married, she tried to get in contact with Ricky to ask if he would relinquish his rights with Lisa so her new husband could adopt her. After trying and failing to reach him for some time, Ricky called her out of the blue. He told her God had told him to call and do what she wanted, which he did. As twisted as poor Ricky's tale is, I think that's a lovely ending.

While working on this book, I learned that Ricky passed away 2005. I was able to make contact with a few of Ricky's swimming teammates, and it was through them that I learned of my brother's fate.

Tug probably never had anything to fear from Ricky. If he hadn't been so averse to all things medical, he might have seen that his son needed the help of a psychiatrist and prevented the terrible tragedy. Regardless, Tug soon found himself the target of my mother, whose hatred for him soon turned to thoughts of murder.

A portrait of my mother.

Mom, Ricky, Kitt, Dad, and Cleet.

Above: My parents on their wedding day, married five weeks after they met. She was still only 17. Below: Me with the pony I bought with my own money. I've rarely been without a horse since. I love them!

Dad holding Kitt and Ricky.

The apartment building my father owned at 2435 3rd Street in Santa Monica still bears his name today!

The infamous *Tugboat*. Can you imagine *this* pulling water skiers?

Even though he did not believe in God, religious themes often appeared in my father's art work.

Self portrait circa 1973.

LOTS OF POISON

Many people talk about murdering their spouses. My mother certainly did. As I grew older, she talked about what it would be like when she finally did her husband in. She talked about how she would cry and mourn for him at the funeral. She talked about all the ways she was going to poison him and make it look like an accident.

She did more than just talk. She really did try to murder my father.

My father became very ill and actually went to a doctor for once when he had a bad kidney infection. It took a lot for my dad to go to a doctor, and the doctor gave him a pill to fight the disease. The pills were the little plastic caplets with medicine inside, and one day, I came home and caught my mother dumping the medicine out of the capsules, refilling them with sugar. Mom was hoping the kidney infection would kill him!

One of my father's weekly activities was to swim the lake near our house. Mom would drive him to Indian Beach and drop him off, then she would drive around to the docks on the other side of the lake to pick him up.

One day I was driving home when I spotted my Dad walking down the side of the road. He was soaking wet, wearing only his swim trunks, and he was bleeding from the knees down. I asked if he wanted a ride, but he refused. "Go tell your mother I am okay," he said. "She's probably worried about me."

When I got to the docks, Mom saw me and became hysterical, bawling her eyes out. When I told her Dad was okay, she actually seemed disappointed. Later on Dad told me that he began to feel sick and dizzy. He cut his swim short pulled himself up on another dock, where he cut his leg. Mom later bragged to me that she had poisoned his tea in hopes of making this his last swim.

I asked her one time why she didn't just divorce him. She clearly hated Dad and wanted to be away from him. She told me that she couldn't just divorce him because, and I quote, "We can't live on half of his money!"

Mom didn't just try to poison Leo's body. She wanted to poison his relationships as well, especially with me. One afternoon a simple conversation about the air conditioning in the house turned into a life-altering ordeal. Mom wanted to turn on the air, and she kept asking if I wanted the air on as well. When I said yes, she went off to talk to Dad.

I don't know what was said in Dad's room, but soon I heard him yelling at her. I got nervous and went off to my room and started cleaning. I was afraid one of them would come after me, and I cleaned so that whatever they were mad about, they wouldn't be able to add a messy room to their complaints.

When Mom returned she said the most awful thing a Mom could tell her child. "Dad is so mad at you," she said. "He doesn't even want to see you. I don't know why, but he's threatening to harm your pets and everything!"

My mother made me deathly afraid of my father that day. I shut myself in my room and stayed there for seven long months.

I was only sixteen and in 10th grade at the time. Mom would help me sneak across the hall to her bathroom, and she would bring me meals in my room. During school hours, I had to have my phone unplugged and my television off. I didn't see my father or the outside of my tiny world for more than half a year.

My exile ended one day when I felt the whole house shake. There was a loud BOOM, and I felt the room tremble. A few seconds later, there was another loud BOOM. Living in California makes you keenly aware that "The Big One" could strike at any time, and I was sure this was an earthquake coming on. I remember saying to myself, "I'm not going to die for that crazy woman," and I ran out of my room, headed for the front of the house.

Before I got there, I saw what was causing the house to shake. My Dad was outside in the car, and he was moving the car back and forth between the trailer with the houseboat and the front porch. The loud BOOMs I felt were my father hitting a support beam on the front porch with the car.

I saw my father, one of the fittest, healthiest men I knew, stagger out of the car and up to the house. I was struck with a sudden fear that he would scream at me. He was mad at me, I thought, and he hadn't seen me for seven months. What would he say?

I was still standing inside the door when he walked in. He looked up, and all he said was, "Hi."

Dad staggered down to his end of the house, where he brushed his teeth and Mom helped him get to bed. It was only 7 PM, and I knew something was very wrong. Dad never went to bed this early. He was always up until 2 AM. When Mom came back out she warned me not to call the police.

I was afraid of her, but I was more afraid of losing my Dad. I called the police.

Fire and medical responders descended on the house. They treated Dad at the house, but as usual, he refused to go to the hospital. I wish he had, because I'm sure a toxicology test would have shown she had poisoned him again.

The next day, things were back to normal. I was allowed back in the kitchen and dining room and the rest of the house, like the last seven months had never happened. I found Dad rummaging through the kitchen, looking for the can of Campbell's Cream of Mushroom Soup. Mom had made him soup the night before, and shortly after, he went out to get dinner for her at her request.

Dad was convinced the soup was poisoned, but in his thinking, the blame lay not with my mother but with Campbell's. My father sealed up the soup can and shipped it off to a laboratory to have it tested. "Those mushrooms were bad," he told me. "I'm going to get that can tested, and when it comes back, I'm going to sue Campbell's!"

I don't doubt the mushrooms were poisoned before they hit the dinner table, but I knew the fault wasn't with Campbell's. When the test came back negative, he decided the lab was in cahoots with Campbell's and faked the test results.

I had a guy friend who did work in the yard for my dad. He told me a story about a time he was talking to my father. Dad was relating one of the many strange tales of sudden illness and near death experiences. My friend told him, "You know she was trying to poison you, right? She brags about it all the time to your daughter."

My father just shook his head. "That just doesn't surprise me."

I eventually went back to school, sometime during my junior year, but with all my absences I never did graduate. I still went on to college and did well. I took a placement test and they admitted me without a diploma.

My mother poisoned every aspect of my adolescence. I was afraid of her, afraid she might do to me the things she did to my father. I was afraid to talk about boys or even wear dresses for fear of her calling me a whore.

One day my mother came to me with a shocking announcement. "Your father and I think you should get married." The young man who did yard work for my father (the same one who told my Dad his wife was trying to murder him, had often asked me out but I was never interested. Turns out he was working on my mother at the same time and prevailed with her where he failed with me. I was still underage, and the idea of dating, much less getting married, was not even on my radar, but Mom had found a way to get rid of me.

"We want you to marry him. He's a nice boy."

I didn't love him, nor did I want to marry him, but I wanted to get away from my mother. I think the feeling was mutual. This was Mom's chance to get rid of me after I betrayed her by calling the cops on her.

Mom went to work planning a wedding for the two of us, and things were going smoothly. Then Mom learned that in the state of California, if you are under age, you have to go through six weeks of counseling before you can get a marriage license. My mother wasn't about to let me speak with any kind of counselor!

Mom did a little more research and discovered that all you need to get married in Arizona is a signature from a parent or guardian. Mom put her blessing in writing and sent us off to Arizona to get married. She then through a "reception" for us in California.

It was a miserable experience. The party was her party, not mine. I didn't get to pick the dress. I didn't get to invite any friends. Mom had plenty of people come by, but they were all her people. There was even a congratulatory telegram from Hulk Hogan.

My marriage only lasted three months. On my 18th birthday, the guy punched me and dislocated my jaw, sending me to the hospital. One of my brothers talked to my husband on the phone and made him promise not to return to the house we shared, a ranch my mom rented for us. We didn't know at the time that the boy was on heroin. That same night he returned to the house and stole most of my stuff, including a 1964 Gibson Les Paul, a gift from a collector who loved to hear me play.

Ten years after our marriage ended, my ex sent me an email apologizing for everything, saying he'd been to jail for his drug addictions and violence. He was in anger management therapy and wanted to ask for forgiveness.

I forgave him and said I was glad he got help, and the two of us became friends again. He told me I was the closest thing to an angel he's ever known, and assured me I didn't deserve anything he had done. Sometimes you need to hear those things.

My ex worked with us a few times in the studio as a music engineer. He even bought me my Jackson V for Christmas a few years ago. He knows it's no substitute for a vintage Les Paul, but I love Jacksons and he knew that. He's fallen prey to some of his old demons in recent years, but I still pray for him all the time.

As soon as I was out of the hospital, Kitt got me and took me to Florida. He took me to a psychiatrist he was seeing, and for the first time in my life, I was told that all of my problems weren't my own doing. It was all my parents' fault.

Three weeks later I returned to California. When I got home, I found out my mother had euthanized my dog. To this day, I can't go anywhere and leave my pets behind because of what that woman did to my dog.

I moved out of the house and began living in my car. Technically, I guess I was homeless, but for the first time in my life, I felt free. Then one day Cleet got in touch with me and told me I needed to come home.

Cleet was home from college, visiting Mom and Dad. He shared something over dinner that caused Dad to get hot. When Dad got angry, Mom got angry at him, and dinner ended with mom firing a gun in the dining room at my father.

After firing the gun, Mom ran outside and paced up and down the street, talking to herself with the gun in hand. The police arrived and took her into custody, but she was only held for 24 hours She was released with her gun after convincing them she was scared of and abused by her "big ex-wrestler husband."

My father was so good to her. He was always kind and gave her everything, but she was a sick and disturbed person. I never once saw my father raise a hand to her, but she would often tell people how afraid she was. She was a liar. Her obsession with made for TV movies made her an expert on plotting a murder and establishing an alibi. It was a game to her, a sick, twisted game that she imagined would come to an end one day with all her friends and neighbors shaking their heads, saying, "She was always so afraid of him, we knew this was coming. That poor, brave woman."

After the shooting they split up for 6 months. It was the only time they ever split up. My father became healthier than he had been in years during that time. He became more active. He had friends and family over to the house. He even got a dog, which was rather funny because my mother always told me he hated animals and that's why I couldn't have a dog.

My mother took me with her when they split, so I heard all of these stories about my father's revival second hand from my aunt. He was healthier, more active, and felt great, but he would also say he was lonely. Loneliness led to forgiveness, and my father took my mother back. It was remarkable how quickly things reverted back to the way they were. The friends weren't allowed over anymore. The family visits were rare. And the dog was quickly gone.

Despite my mother's best efforts, my father remained close to a handful of friends from his wrestling days thanks to the Cauliflower Alley Club. Dad loved to make the annual trek to their convention in Studio City and catch up with some of the boys to talk about their glory days, and everyone loved it when his lordship graced their presence.

"We used to tease him a lot about his hair," says Karl Lauer, former president of the CAC. "We joked that he had to go to the salon to get his color right and get all those curls in his hair. Truth is, his was all natural. It was Gorgeous George who needed the bleach and the stylists."

The CAC was dad's chance to catch up with old friends. Mike Mazurki, Vic Christy, and Ted Christy were just a few of the old timers who always made dad feel welcome. Dad also took the opportunity to bring his art work along to some of the conventions.

"Mike Mazurki always asked him, 'Why won't you put me in any paintings?'" says Lauer. "Carlton would tell him, 'You're just too damn ugly!'"

Lauer noted that my father's art work was always well received, but there was one painting that stood out for him more than any other. "It's the one with the guys huddled around the TV, watching wrestling. That's one of the few paintings that connects to wrestling, and even though there's no wrestling in it. It captures the 1950s wrestling world so perfectly. The looks on these guys' faces, looking at the television, it tells a story. They worked hard all day long, and the just couldn't wait to get home, grab a beer in the kitchen, and watch some wrestling. He sold the original to one of the Cauliflower Alley members for $500. I can only imagine what it's worth today."

The Boob Tube, Karl Lauer's favorite piece my dad's. Below: *Street of Forgotten Dreams.* This was always hanging over my father's king sized bed in his room.

My favorite, hanging in my dining room. It's called *1900 Yesterday*, like the song. My father liked hauntingly sad songs.

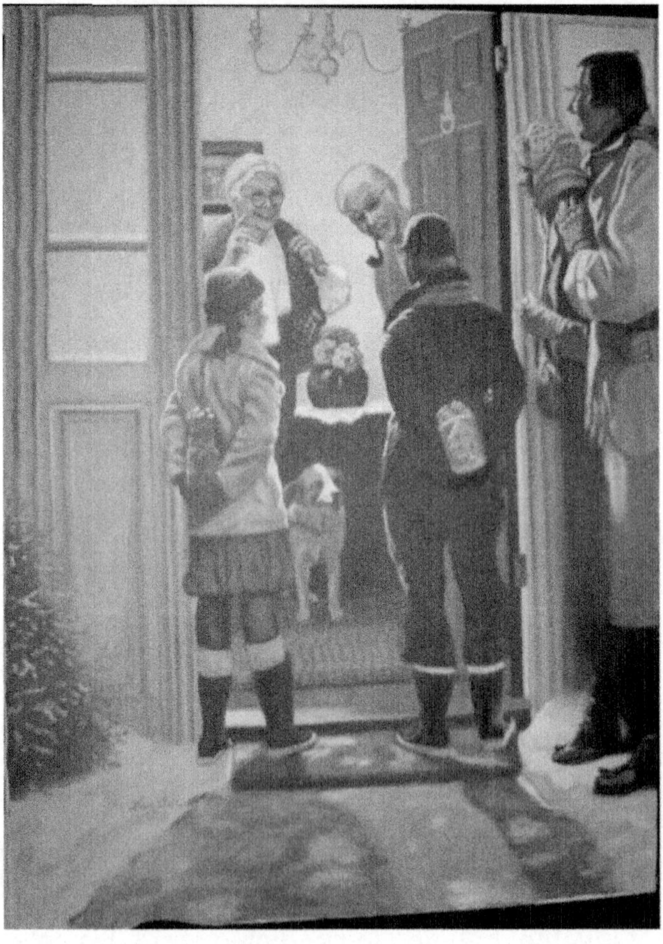

Above: Dad donated this painting of a Raiders vs. Seahawks game to the local Lions Club for a charity auction. Below: A very late photo of my Dad before he died.

Me at age seventeen, writing deep thoughts. Or some heavy metal polka.

DRAMA AND TRAGEDY

My mother loved drama. She loved to create it, and she loved to be in the center of it. But in my family she was never alone in her love for drama. My aunt and my father were both capable of drama just as much as she was.

Mom actually left dad for a period of six months. Dad put a hold on her access to their money while she was away, so she took him to court. Mom went out and got a job at a Jack in the Box restaurant so she could come in and plead her case to the judge. "I'm so destitute, I went out an got a job at a fast food restaurant!"

Not to be outdone, my father came into the courtroom fashionably late, explaining to the judge that he was only detained because he was "busy caring for the sick, for the needy, and for the homeless!" He was in his 70s at the time, but that day before a gallery of witnesses, I got to see my father in the form that made him a stand out wrestler thirty years prior.

My parents thrived on courtroom drama. It was one of the few things they were able to enjoy together. They were constantly ending up in court with tenants and former tenants from their apartment buildings over one thing or another. My parents brought a dramatic flair to the courtroom every chance they got.

Mom had one particular gimmick she used in court all the time. If she was the defendant, she showed up late feigning nausea, pretending to be pregnant. Shameful? Yes. But it worked more often than not, and Mom reveled in the attention she received.

My Aunt Paula got into the act during one particularly strange trial. A tenant sued my parents after they gave him an eviction notice. The tenant's complaint: they pushed the written notice through the keyhole in the door and poked him in the eye, causing permanent damage.

Aunt Paula figured one strange tale deserved another, so when she stood up in court, she regaled the judge with the most elaborate tale of woe she could possibly spin. She told the judge how this "miserable little man" in a "smoking jacket with a telescoping cigarette holder" harassed them as they tried to serve him legal notice.

Mom stirred up a great deal of drama with her spending habits as well. Mom could easily drop $100-200 in a day, even back in the 70s. Dad would try to curb her spending, but she would find ways around it.

I had a beautiful Pontiac Trans Am car. One day I went out to get in my car and it was just gone. I ran inside the house and called the cops to report my car was stolen. The police told me that no, my car had not been stolen; it was repossessed.

Without my knowing, my mother went out an took a loan against my car! The car was paid for, and I owned the title free and clear. But I had to call my father and ask for $600 just to get my car back.

Dad, unfortunately, was little help. Dad didn't like my car; he never understood the importance of things like, you know, aerodynamics. He offered to buy me a brand new one, but I insisted I wanted my car back.

I demanded to talk to Mom, since she was the cause of all the trouble in the first place. Dad told me, "Mom can't come to the phone right now. She's had a stroke."

I kid you not, a few days later, I dropped by the house. Mom was sitting up in bed, and as soon as she saw it was me, she began talking like she couldn't move one side of her face.

This kind of fakery and play acting was always going on in my family. And that is why to this day, I really don't know the full story of the illness that took my father's life.

I called Dad up one day to ask for some money. I had an opportunity to buy a house, and I wanted him to go in with me, 50/50. Dad replied that, no, he could not loan me any money at that moment. "Don't tell your mother," he said. "But I went to donate some blood today, to help the poor and homeless. They told me that I have leukemia."

Right away, Dad told me not to tell my mother. We both knew this was the kind of thing that, if true, would thrill her. For the next year, he kept talking about his diagnosis to me, but he would never say anything to my Mom. She suspected something was up, and when she caught us whispering, she'd demand to know what we were talking about. We never said a word.

About a year later, my mom came to me. "Your father has leukemia."

"I know," I said. "He told me a year ago."

"No, that's not possible!" she said. "He just now found out!"

I wish I could tell you who was telling the truth, my mother or my father. Mom was convinced that he had lied to her for a year, and in making up the lie, he had jinxed himself into getting leukemia. My mother was extremely superstitious like that.

The alternative is to believe my father really did know he had leukemia for a year and never treated it. As I have stated, my father never liked going to the doctor, but after mom told me about the diagnosis, he began going regularly.

My father went into a very rapid decline. Over the next eight months, his body wasted away, and he became very weak. It was heartbreaking to watch. My father was so dedicated to staying healthy. He had vowed as a child never to be weak again, and yet, he couldn't stop the decline.

Dad was very lonely in those days. Remember that job Mom got at Jack in the Box when she left? She decided she liked it, and she stayed on for twenty years. I suspect it gave her an opportunity to hang around with young people who could hook her up with drugs.

Mom was never around, and she did her best to keep other people away. She would tell me that my father hated me and didn't want to see me. She lied and told my Aunt Paula that the local pastor was dropping in on my father every day. My father was getting no such visitors. For one thing, he was an atheist. And for another, Mom kept everyone she could away from his bedside.

Paula discovered that my dad was not getting all of his medication. She went to my mother and offered to pick them up, but my mother blew her off. "He doesn't know anything. He has all he needs."

"He's lonely," said Aunt Paula. "Maybe you could rent out a room, just so he has someone to talk to."

My mother's personality flipped on a dime, as I had witnessed so many times in my life. "Rent out your own f—ing rooms and mind your own business!"

I hate to keep saying, this, but it's the honest truth. Mom was just waiting for him to pass. She couldn't wait. "I'll shed a few tears at the funeral when he's gone, but after that, life will be so much better."

Eight months after my mother told me my dad was sick, he passed away at the age of 74. He died just days before Christmas. My mother celebrated. She threw half his stuff in the garbage. She even bought me a brand new car. Small consolation for a girl who just lost her father.

My father's pain was mercifully at an end, but it continued for me. My mother told me she held a pillow over his face as he lay in the hospital bed gasping for air so he'd stop wanting to leave the hospital and come home. She told me she was "tired of taking care of an old man." She said if someone had caught her, she'd cry and say it was a mercy killing. For all I know, this whole story is a lie; she almost never told the truth about anything.

I don't even recall where I spent that Christmas that year. My life became a blur. I was probably at some friend's house, feeling like an intruder, wondering if my mom would go to jail and wondering if my dad died because it was his time.

I didn't attend the funeral. I was afraid I might snap, watching my mom cry crocodile tears and putting on the show of grief she had long prepared for. I wished it was her being laid in that grave. I didn't want to feel those feelings, so I went to a burger place and sat there drinking milkshakes.

After his funeral, my dad's cousin Stan came up to our house. Mom was hard at work throwing away the things my father loved while I was trying to hide them away to keep. When she saw Stan, she thought he was my father's ghost limping up the driveway and freaked out. She let him stay with us a while, but immediately became neglectful and abusive to him.

Stan had some medical problems of his own. I had my driver's license so I would drive him to Loma Linda Hospital for his medical care. We took many drives together, and I loved his company, but the good times didn't last long.

I was out of town when Stan injured himself, burning his leg with hot coffee. He asked Mom to drive him to the hospital. She refused, saying, "I got rid of one old man! I'm not going to be stuck taking care of another!" I was so sad he left. Once again I was isolated alone with her.

Showing off some of Lord Carlton's fineries today.

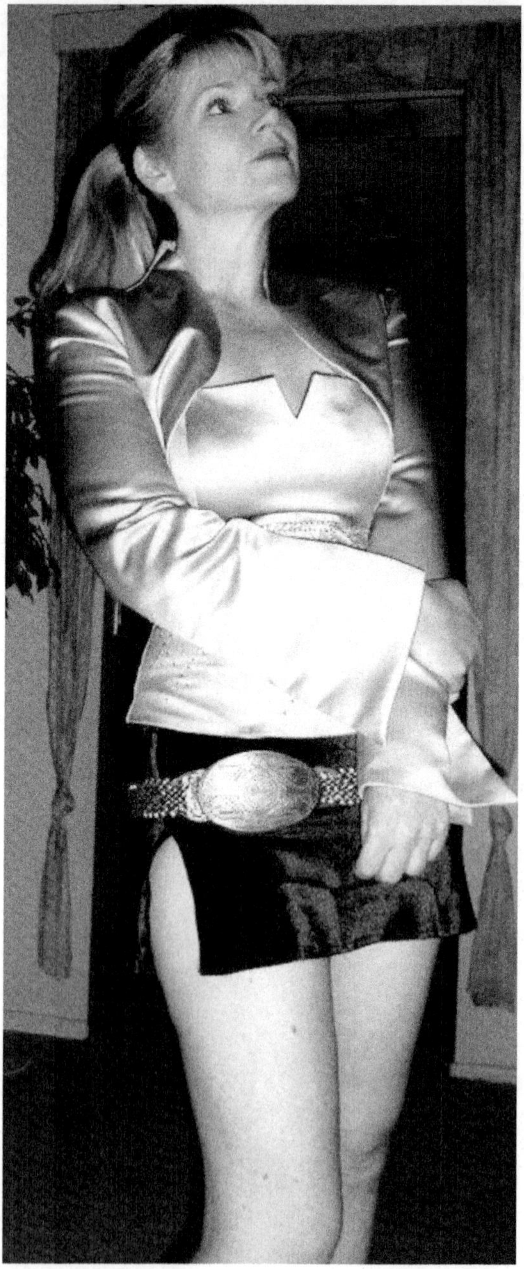

LORD CARLTON'S LEGACY

Yes, that's me on the left. I wouldn't be Lord Carlton's daughter if I didn't try the fight game at least once, right?

It was 2009 when I was asked to be a ring girl for a boxing show. My mechanic's son was a rising star in boxing. He knew my background, and he begged me to do it. so I did. I don't remember the name of the boxing promotion, but at least there's a photo to capture the memory.

When I was 16, some of my dad's friends asked if I wanted to be a ring girl for a wrestling promotion. My dad asked me if I was interested, but before I could answer, Mom jumped in and said I wasn't allowed.

That same year Mom tried to marry me off to the son of some business partner of theirs because he owned tons of real estate. I remember being horrified and my mother countering with, "But he drives your favorite car, a Lamborghini!"

After my father passed away, my mother began to drink and smoke heavily. She took handfuls of Vivarin and ran from morning until night. Yet in spite of her reckless living, she lived more years than my health-conscious father.

At the time we first published this book, my mom was living in a nursing home in Southern California. Her health was in rapid decline, and it was getting harder and harder to understand her. Oddly enough, her

Catholic upbringing was becoming crystal clear in those later years. She would randomly interjet "Hail Mary!" into her sentences as she spoke in an almost manic manner.

I've read a great deal in recent years about Stockholm Syndrome, the attachment bond that hostages form with kidnappers in high tension situations. I've become convinced that was at work in my relationship with my mother. I moved to Northern California to get some space between us when she was living in a Southern California nursing home, yet in spite of all the terrible things Mom did to my Dad and to me, I felt guilty not being near her.

I called her up one day to check on her. It had been at least a week since I had last spoken to her, so of course, I was feeling guilty over that. When the nurses put her on the phone, she was incapable of speaking. I could hear her trying, and breathing, as the nurse held the phone to her ear. The nurse told me she was smiling, happy to hear my voice, happy to hear me say I loved her.

After that call, she passed away. It was like she was waiting to hear from me before she left this world for the next. I pray she is as peace in God's loving arms.

That may seem surprising to some people, wishing peace on a person who caused so much pain, but I know that many of my mother's issues were beyond her control. While I was raised to believe that seeing a doctor or counselor of any kind was wrong. I now see very clearly the need for medical and psychological treatment. Had my father and mother not been so averse to such things, I can't help but wonder if life would have turned out differently for my older brother and his mother. Mental illness is a very real thing.

There's no shame in seeking treatment when you need it, but shame to those who would make a person feel guilty over seeking such treatment.

I've made a fresh start here, and some good friends, but I find it hard to trust in other people. My mother has something to do with that. So do two marriages that crumbled and fell apart. I'm so used to the false front that my mother put on, I keep waiting for someone to snap.

So far, so good.

Today I live in the country on a beautiful old farm. Think of it as Green Acres, but with a Hungarian rock star instead of a Hungarian diva. I take care of the livestock. I work. I create music and mayhem whenever I can. I've been through a lot of changes the last few years, but I have my faith, and that gives me peace.

I can't tell you how hard it was to grow up with the absence of any faith in God in my house. When you're in a chaotic environment such as the one that I knew, and there's no reason to hope for something better, it really leads you to some dark places.

By the time I was 12, I had no siblings left in the house. Both of my grandmothers had long passed away, and we lived in a private community. It was a very isolated environment. The school I attended was in the next town. Most of the girls from my community were wealthy and conceited, and very morally corrupt. I was tormented by them, and could not seek help from a drunken mother who also denied me access to my father.

I wish more counselors would be trained to recognize parental alienation and call it what it is: child abuse. The children who suffer from parental alienation need help, but so do the parents, who need counseling to get to the root of why they demonize the other parent.

I would often find my mother up late, drunk, watching horror movies. She was deeply superstitious, obsessed with horror and gothic culture, and would tell me she was from a long line of witches. My choices, as they were laid out, were to deny the existence of God and be an atheist like my father, or worship the "dark side" and be like my mother. I felt comfortable with neither.

That's not to say I grew up completely absent of a moral code. My father instilled a very Christian moral ethic within me, minus the "why" of Christianity. I was confident in my sense of right and wrong, but that often led to more confusion. I respected the morals and values he taught me, but applying them in the world while denying God made for some bad decisions. Friends would ask me to join in things that I didn't want to do, and I would tell them no. My friends would mock me and ask why. "Do you believe in God?"

"No," I said, "I don't."

"Then why not?"

I was torn. I didn't want to do something I felt was wrong, but these were my friends, and I was just as fearful of being called self-righteous and stuck up. Imagine all your friends pushing you to have sex with people, do drugs, and do things you knew deep inside were wrong to a degree that their behavior frightened you. Imagine your friends accusing you of being the bad one and the hypocrite for not going along. That's what it's like to try and stand up to peer pressure without Christianity as your shield. You can't defend yourself, or be wise enough to avoid them, because you can't declare that you'd rather follow God's word than the world.

My father said people who believe in God are mentally ill, so of course I couldn't be friends with people like that. I chose to be around people who laughed at such things, but those people never shared my values. My childhood was confusing, and then that bled into my adult life with much turmoil, bad decisions, and abuse from bad people.

One day, early in my adulthood, I got a hold of a Bible. I had never seen or read any of the Bible; it was strictly forbidden in our house. But as I began to read the Bible, things finally clicked for me. My father never believed in God or Jesus, yet it was in God and Jesus that I found the reason to believe all the things he taught me. The moral code my father gave me finally found bedrock in the Word of God. And that, more than anything, is why Lord Carlton's daughter gave her life to Christ.

Becoming a Christian has not been an easy road. Many of the friends I've made who profess themselves to be Christians act as if they are better than you. They nitpick everything you do, like cussing, and use that against you. They tell you that you are not a real Christian, kicking you down while making themselves appear better than you instead of trying to raise you up. "Friends" like these certainly help me to understand why so many new (and old) Christians soon become ex-Christians, because who wants to associate with people who treat you like garbage?

You also lose a lot of the old friends, the ones who led you astray because they didn't believe in God. They think you've gone mad and end up leaving you, which can be sad but also a blessing. Much as I hate to see people go, sometimes you have to break those ties if you truly want to make changes in your life.

I often wish I could have had faith in my younger days. If someone had given me a Bible at an earlier age and asked me to read it through, or tried explaining it sensibly, I think I would have responded to that. But I am grateful I came to my faith when I did, and I wouldn't trade it for anything.

There are many "what ifs" in my life story. What if the school I attended cared enough to investigate all my absences and so-called sicknesses? What if someone had been able to get me into counseling? Maybe my life would have been easier. Then again, maybe the hard road was necessary to lead me where I am today.

Perhaps God knew I needed to go through so many challenges. Perhaps the hard times were his way of preparing me to know Him and to help others. Perhaps that was my intended path so I could see it in others and reach out with kindness instead of self righteous indignation.

Life was not easy growing up the daughter of Lord Leslie Carlton and his second bride, but in spite of all the badness, things worked out the way God intended. I believe that same happy ending is possible for anyone. If you are open to receive the message through all the fog, through all the distractions, through all the darkness, He will meet you there, right where you are.

I often wonder what my father would say if he were alive today. I can tell you right off the bat, he would hate what's become of his beloved Democratic

Party. He was a left wing liberal, a strong supporter of men like Kennedy and Johnson, but I doubt he'd approve of the party, or the government in general, as it stands today.

I think Dad's favorite politician would be Vladimir Putin. Putin's an old KGB man, a throwback to a bygone era and a time when my father truly admired the Soviet experiment. I think Dad would enjoy the zaniness of the Russian leader with his shirtless poses and his remarkable candor.

It's hard to say how Dad would feel about today's wrestling scene. Most of the old timers are pretty sour when it comes to modern wrestling. They long for the days when wrestling was "real" in the minds of the fans, when kayfabe still ruled the industry, and when cartoon characters were the exception rather than the norm. My father was old school in many ways, but as Lord Leslie Carlton, he's the spiritual ancestor to the crazy caricatures that dominate today's wrestling world. He might hate it, but he'd have only himself to blame.

I can't imagine he would be happy with his daughter trekking off to church every Sunday, but I hope he would see that the faith I have is an extension of the moral code he instilled in me. I hope, too, that he would see some of himself in me, the same Hungarian spirit that led him and his parents into the spotlight of show business. I am sure he would be proud.

I'm also sure if he saw me singing on stage or performing on film, he'd find some way to barge in on my act, to steal one more second in the spotlight, to perform for the rock fans the same way he did for the wrestling fans, the galleries in courtrooms, and the national TV audiences that made him a star.

What else would you expect from His Lordship, the hero of Her Majesty's armed forces, the inimitable Lord Leslie Carlton?

ACKNOWLEDGEMENTS

We would like to thank the people who helped to make this book a reality.

Thanks to Karl Lauer, Johnny and Rosemary Andriolo, and Lou D'Elia for sharing their personal accounts of the great Lord Carlton, in and out of the ring.

Thank you to Dale Pierce for pointing us in the direction of the Phil Melby match in Arizona, 1958.

Thank you to Myrtle Casey for the photos of Tug Carlson vs. her husband Jim Casey.

Thank you to Jim Oetkins for photos.

Thank you as well to the late, great J. Michael Kenyon for his expertise and his willingness to fact check the book.

Thank you to Ally LaBar and John Cosper, Sr., for their assistance in editing the book.

A number of websites proved to be invaluable in the writing of this book as we looked for details about His Lordship's wrestling career. In no particular order, we'd like to thank the people behind:

Newspapers.com

Online World of Wrestling

Wrestlingdata.com

Wrestlingclassics.com

Slam! Sports

House of Deception

A few stories, including the many pranks of Vic Christy, were found in Joe Jares's classic *Whatever Happened to Gorgeous George?* The book is available through Crowbar Press and is a must read for anyone who appreciates the golden age of wrestling. It will give you a richer appreciation for many of the characters and themes seen even in today's wrestling.

ABOUT THE AUTHORS

K.K. Herzbrun is the daughter of Leo Whippern, better known to the wrestling world as Lord Leslie Carlton. She curates a huge collection of photos, robes, art work, and other memorabilia from her father's life, things she hid from and saved from her mother after Lord Carlton's passing. She currently lives a rock and roll version of *Green Acres* on a farm in Northern California where she ride horses, enjoy the outdoors, and writes music.

John Cosper is an author, wrestling historian, and blogger. His previous books on wrestling include *Bluegrass Brawlers: The Story of Professional Wrestling in Louisville*; *Eat Sleep Wrestle*; *Louisville's Greatest Show*; and *Don't Call Me Fake: The Real Story of "Dr. D" David Schultz*. He writes about wrestling's past and present at eatsleepwrestle.com. He lives in Indiana with his wife and two kids.